Thomas S. Owens

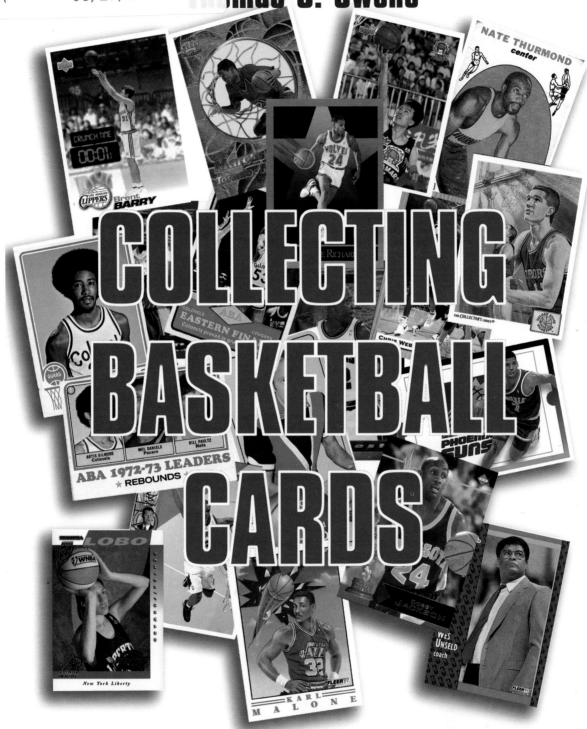

COLLECTING BASKETBALL CARDS

The Millbrook Press   Brookfield, Connecticut

to Diana Star Helmer

and

Jean Reynolds,

two star teammates

The author wishes to thank the following card companies
for their assistance and cooperation in providing illustrative
materials for the interior and cover of this book: Beckett Publications/
Taiwan Cardwon Co.; Collector's Edge of Tennessee, Inc.;
Fleer/Skybox Corp.; Pacific Trading Cards, Inc.;
Pinnacle Trading Card Company; The Score Board, Inc.;
Topps Company, Inc.; Upper Deck Company

Library of Congress Cataloging-in-Publication Data
Owens, Tom, 1960–
Collecting basketball cards/by Thomas S. Owens.
p.   cm.
Includes bibliographical references and index.
Summary: Provides practical advice on building a basketball card
collection, covering such topics as buying and trading cards,
as well as grading and preserving them.
ISBN 0–7613–0418–5 (lib. bdg.)
1. Basketball cards—Collectors and collecting—Juvenile literature.
[1. Basketball cards—Collectors and collecting.]   I. Title.
GV885.15.O94   1998
796.323'0973'075—dc21 98-4432
CIP   AC

Published by The Millbrook Press, Inc.
2 Old New Milford Road
Brookfield, Connecticut 06804

CONTENTS

ROUND BALL, RECTANGLE CARDS

To understand the history of basketball cards, you need to know the history of basketball. That history stretches beyond last year's NBA champs, the debut of Michael Jordan, or even the birth of the National Basketball Association.

The game of basketball was born in 1891, in a YMCA in Springfield, Massachusetts. Dr. James Naismith taught physical education there. He created a new way to keep his students active: a game in which players tried to throw a ball into peach baskets that the janitor nailed to the gym's balcony railing.

Just two years later, the first players were playing for pay. But there weren't many professional teams at first. Teams had to "barnstorm," traveling to find opposing teams willing to host them. Simply finding a place to play regularly was a challenge for those earliest pros. The New York Original Celtics

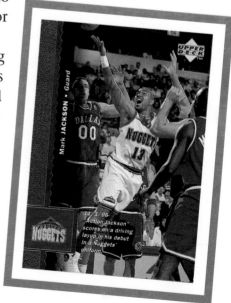

For the first time in its 1996–97 set, Upper Deck revealed the origin of photos used with dated captions on card fronts. Previously, collectors studying card photos had to guess the time and place of the picture. (Copyright © the Upper Deck Company)

became one of the first to find a home—and a constant ticket-buying following—in Manhattan.

CARDS WITHOUT CARDBOARD?

Basketball remained mostly a student interest until 1925. In fact, the earliest basketball "cards" come from a 1910 set called College Athlete Felts. This multisport set of 270 felt squares featured 20 entries of basketball moves, showing unidentified, generic players. One year later, Murad Cigarettes put out a similar multisport set. Four entries recognized individual colleges, although no special player was noted. But Murad's 1911 cards were the first actually printed on cardboard, similar to the collectibles chased by fans today.

The American Basketball League formed in 1925. This organized group of teams only lasted until 1931. The Great Depression had begun, the economic collapse of the United States. But the Celtics continued, now a mainstay transplanted to Boston. Four of the team's stars were featured in the Goudey "Sports Kings" set in 1933. Cards of Eddie Burke, Joe Lapchick, Nat Holman, and Ed Wachter became a basketball hobby first. Now cards existed of specific players, just like in other sports. These were also the first basketball cards to come from gum packs.

Still, basketball had to share the card spotlight with other sports. Forty-four of Goudey's cards pictured athletes from other sports.

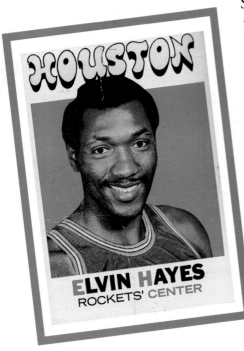

Even in 1974–75, Topps still seemed worried about protests from the NBA. To avoid showing team logos, players posed wearing their jerseys turned backward. Topps added game-action backgrounds to make posed portraits more exciting. (Copyright © Topps Company, Inc.)

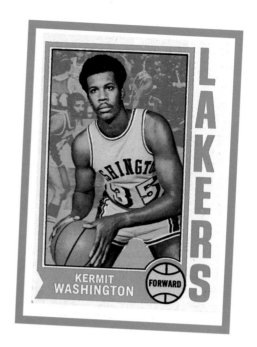

The National Basketball League began in 1937. For 12 years, teams moved from city to city, looking for fan support. Many teams failed. In 1949, six still-active teams joined the Basketball Association of America, a lesser-known group that had been playing since 1946. The new merger created the National Basketball Association on August 3, 1949.

MANY SEASONS, FEW SETS

The new league formed just in time to celebrate the first-ever all-basketball set. Bowman, a Philadelphia-based company, created the 72-card set in 1948. Actually, only 60 different players got cards in this set, each measuring $2\frac{1}{16}$ inches by $2\frac{1}{2}$ inches. A dozen cards diagrammed basketball plays for young player-fans. Player photos were black and white, but Bowman printed a solid color background for each. That was the plan, but some cards have plain backgrounds because the printer ran out of colored ink!

Some card backs included a mail-in offer. Send in 10 cents and three wrappers, and you could get two different felt letters to press onto your sweater. You could choose any letters, to signify your favorite school team.

Topps' first version of basketball cards came in 1948, too. While it wasn't a hoops-only set, six college pictures appeared in

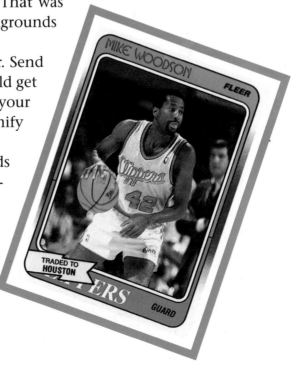

Fleer, for its 1988–89 set, didn't pretend to have up-to-the-minute photographs. Even though Woodson was traded from the Clippers, the company didn't have time to picture him in his new uniform. (Copyright © Fleer/SkyBox Corp.)

the 252-card "Magic Photos" set featuring movie performers and stars from various sports. Along with five individual cards of All-American stars, one card was a game-action scene entitled "Manhattan Beats Dartmouth."

These cards are far from the traditional designs of today. Each "Magic Photo" measured ⅞ of an inch by 1⁷⁄₁₆ inches. Card fronts were blank. It was the collector's job to "develop" the picture by holding the card to sunlight—or using a damp cloth! However, Topps' choice to include basketballers among stars of boxing, baseball, and other higher-profile sports gave collectors hope for the future. So did Bowman's all-basketball set.

TOPPS TIPS OFF

But Bowman didn't put out a basketball set the next year—or the next. Hopes for another Bowman set died in 1955, when Topps bought the competing company and put it out of business. Topps waited two more years before producing the second national all-basketball set in 1957. All 80 cards depicted individual players. These cards measured up to today's standard—2½ by 3½ inches—and included some full-photo game-action shots. A six-pack sold for a nickel. But though the company made a three-card advertising panel promising next year's set, there wasn't a "next year" until 1969.

Fleer was the basketball hobby's next one-year wonder. This company printed a 66-card set for the 1961–62 season. The first 44 cards in the set were standard poses. The rest of the set included action shots, featuring players pictured previously in the set. That allowed Fleer to pay fewer players to be on their cards!

Hobbyists have countless theories about why the first NBA card sets didn't succeed. Card companies are often blamed for giving up too quickly. No matter what the explanation, the National Basketball League didn't become a regular attraction for card collectors until it was 20 years old.

A SECRET SET?

Even then, Topps didn't rush back into the basketball-card market. The company started slowly, preparing a 22-card "test" set in 1968. Card fronts used black-and-white photos, including the player's name, team, and height. Card backs were puzzle pieces that would form a huge picture of Wilt Chamberlain. Price guides list the 22-card set at $12,000 and up. Why?

Few test-issue cards were supposed to reach public collections. Unlike the promotional cards that are given away at collectibles shows today, these cards were supposed to stay in company hands. Collectors think that these rare cards were probably "discovered" only because employees brought home extras, or the company's castoffs were uncovered in the garbage.

That test set convinced Topps to return to basketball in a big way in 1969. These cards measured 2½ by 4¹¹⁄₁₆ inches. Today, some collectors call the oversized issues "tall boys." The 1969–70 set was only 99 cards (98 players and one checklist). Card backs featured a one-sentence bit of player trivia

Topps issued a 99-card set for the 1969–70 season. One pack contained 10 cards and a miniposter, all for a dime! The cardmaker hadn't tried basketball cards in ten years, not since its first set in 1957–58. (Copyright © Topps Company, Inc.)

It's easy to imagine what it would be like to collect a particular, spectacular basketball card. A harder task is to imagine what it feels like to *be* that basketball card.

Leo "Crystal" Klier (pronounced CLEAR) was card number 24 in the 1948 Bowman set, the first-ever cards that were nationally distributed in packs. Born in 1923, Klier played pro ball from 1946–50. What does he remember about being one of the first stars on cardboard?

"I have grandchildren who collect cards, and it's a thrill for them!" he says. "Even after 50 years, I still receive an occasional letter from someone requesting a signature on a Bowman card. I am pleased that young people show an interest. I still have a few cards of my own. The cards that people ask me to sign are like new...excellent quality!

"Being part of the Bowman set was okay. Since I have a few of my cards, my portrait is forever in my memory. However, I think improvement could have been made. For instance, I played most of my time with a crew-cut hairstyle. The picture on the card does not represent this fact. My family and friends like to remember my playing days...the card helps. [There was] little reaction by other players [to the cards]. Things were really low-key in those days.

"Commercialism and a strong economy, plus the growth of basketball internationally, have put a new face on the card game. Life has become a 'runaway' train. I was never contacted by anyone concerning issuance of a personal card. In my day, I never took a plane; it was either automobile or train. The league was restricted geographically and card collecting was pretty much grounded, too!"

Bill Thieben, born in 1935, played in 1956–57 for Fort Wayne. His career concluded after the 1957–1958 season with Detroit. He is card number 20 in the 1957–58 Topps set.

"I remember coming home from practice one day and saying to my wife, 'We are going out for dinner tonight! Some bubble-gum company gave me a check for 25 dollars to be on a picture card.' We did, in fact, go out for dinner in one of the best restaurants in Fort Wayne, Indiana, on that check and still came home with a ten-dollar bill. . . . Salaries were not too crazy in those days.

"I do not think there was much of a reaction among the guys on the team. We just took it in stride and went about the business of playing basketball."

But Thieben's story picks up again years later. "There is a little neighborhood pub in Syracuse (home of the Syracuse Nationals at that time), and my son was there with friends. They all got to talking about the old NBA when my son said, 'My dad is on a bubble-gum card.' Well, the pub owner happened to have my card, and my son won a 50-dollar bet. [That's] double what I got to appear on the card to begin with!"

Unlike the league's pioneers, more of today's players chase their own cards. Jason Kidd is one of the NBA's best-known collectors. (Copyright and courtesy Fleer/SkyBox Corp.)

my card. The fact that Edwardsville, Illinois, was such a small town, I thought the townspeople would get a kick out of [each Fleer card listing the player's hometown]."

Walter Dukes, born in 1930, became card number 11 in the 1961–62 Fleer set. One of the early 7-footers, he was an NBA player from 1955 to 1963.

"Since I was five years old, basketball cards and other sports cards have always been involved in my life, as a child who played with them, as a player with the Harlem Globetrotters, and presently, with my children, who frequently show my grandchildren the old and new form of such. The cards prior to the 1961–62 Fleer set [picturing Dukes], ignited my appetite as well as all my childhood friends', for numerous sports which I participated in simply because of the knowledge of these cards.

"Fleer's cards motivated us to think of sports and to compete at all levels. Significantly, it helped me to obtain a level of contentment and love [for the game from] early childhood to date.

"I have fond memories and heartwarming thoughts of each time I recall a card, a personality and their background with my own activities, which culminated in being placed in the 1961–62 set of cards."

Earl Shannon, born in 1921, played in the pros from 1946 to 1949. He is card number 22 in the 1948 Bowman set.

"When I first learned that Bowman had published a card with my photo thereon, I was surprised but proud. If I recall, the photo they used was one taken for publicity purposes by the Providence Steamrollers [team]. I am not aware of any involvement of Bowman personnel and I never did receive any consideration of any [kind], including copies of the card."

Don Ohl, born in 1936, was card number 33 in the 1961–62 Fleer set. He played in the NBA from 1960 to 1970.

"I don't recall for sure [the money offered], maybe around $500. There were no agents and no players association that would suggest royalties. My kids did enjoy the free gum samples [from Fleer]. Fleer used a [Pistons team supplied] public-relations picture on dressed up with a humorous bit of artwork. These cartoon biographies were a special Topps trademark—but the company didn't stop there. A 10-cent pack would yield 10 cards, a stick of gum, and a "ruler." The ruler was a folded paper poster, with a cartoon drawing of a certain NBA player next to a tape measure, indicating his looming height. A total of 24 ruler-posters were available. This set within a set was known as an "insert." To get collectors to buy more packs of cards, Topps would insert an extra bonus of some sort in each package.

Such touches made collectors think that Topps would rule the basketball-card world forever. And the company was essentially unchallenged through 1981–82. But when the popularity of the NBA dipped, so did card sales, and Topps gave up its license to make NBA cards.

Ten years later basketball was on top again, and so were basketball cards. But the popularity of the game and its cards haven't always grown side by side. One of the best ways to see and appreciate the growth of the game is to study past cards and their struggles for acceptance.

THE HOBBY'S WHO'S WHO

Every team has to start somewhere. When the Toronto Raptors and the Vancouver Grizzlies became new NBA teams for the 1995–96 season, each Canadian club built its roster by drafting players from other teams. They decided what kind of players they needed, and how to get those players.

As you build your basketball-card collection, you have to decide the "what" and "how" of your personal collection. You should know what types of cards you want before deciding how to get more cards through buying, trading, and selling.

Trying to collect one of everything, any card ever made, would be terrifically difficult and very expensive.

Were these basketball cards? Collectors still argue over whether the 1996 Upper Deck "Space Jam" set is a basketball collectible or a non-sports issue. Because players like Jordan and Charles Barkley weren't shown in NBA uniforms, some hobbyists weren't interested. Upper Deck sent out this "promo" card, numbered "SJ1" to dealers previewing the set. (Copyright © the Upper Deck Company)

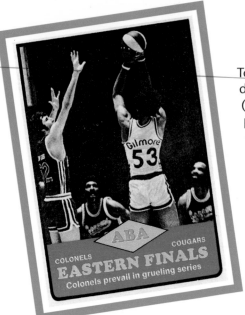

Topps did little bragging in the 1970s. This 1973–74 card doesn't identify the company, expect for a T.C.G. copyright (short for Topps Chewing Gum). Also, the year of the ABA playoff isn't mentioned on the card either, frustrating students of basketball history. A peek at *The Basketball Encyclopedia* solved the riddle. (Copyright © Topps Company, Inc.)

Many collectors choose sets made by a particular card company. Other collectors don't want to get tied down to one manufacturer. Instead, they seek only special types of cards.

Pick up a leading price-guide magazine like *Beckett Basketball Card Monthly*, and here are some of the card categories you'll see:

SEMISTARS

These are the almost-famous types of players. They are the promising players with struggling teams, or teams in cities with less media coverage. Any player for a team in New York, Los Angeles, or Chicago is likely to be swamped by reporters who report on the player's every thought and move, good or bad. But a player in a lesser spot (like Minneapolis) or an area stuffed with sports teams (like Sacramento) can be ignored for years.

Likewise, a player on a great team might be overlooked. Imagine playing next to Michael Jordan, hoping for a share of recognition. When a team has one huge star, that fame tends to hide the talents and personalities of teammates.

Sometimes, a semistar card may represent a player with rising fame. Or the semistar card may symbolize a player with declining, or uncertain, acclaim. For instance, in 1997, Golden State's Latrelle Sprewell was the team's leading scorer. His cards

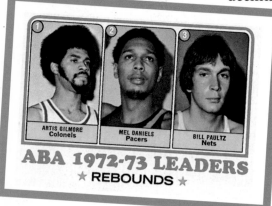

Topps pioneered the idea of "Leaders" cards. This card from the 1973–74 set is collectible because of the popularity of the long-gone American Basketball Association, and because of Artis Gilmore's rise to the Hall of Fame. The triple-photo cards in 1970s' Topps sets became most popular when more-famous players were shown. (Copyright © Topps Company, Inc.)

were limited to semistar status, due to the team's 1–13 mid-season record. Then Sprewell was suspended by the league for one year, after brawling with head coach P. J. Carlesimo. Next, Sprewell made history by becoming the first NBA player ever to have a contract voided for insubordination. In other words, Sprewell was fired. Once his future with the Warriors, and maybe the entire NBA, seemed unsure, you could bet that his cards wouldn't gain in value soon.

STARS

Call them superstar cards or star cards. Either name is a safe call for strong value.

ROOKIES

A rookie card always holds this label. Players may go hot and cold in terms of popularity. Their cards might rise and dip in terms of holding semistar and star value. But a rookie card is always a rookie card, whether its player is called a star, a semistar, or a bench-warmer.

However, what exactly is a rookie card? There's still debate in many hobby circles. The usual definition is a player's first card in a standard set with national distribution. If the Spurs are featured on a regional set only in Texas, any first-year player included in that regional set wouldn't get "rookie card" status in the hobby. The card has to be available nationally. The tricky part is: The card does not have to be issued during the player's rookie season. Sometimes, the card may come out before the start of a player's NBA career (for example, in the case of a "draft-pick" card). Still, an "official" rookie card has to be a regular card within the set, not part of a team photo or other specialty card.

The hobby debate continues about what makes a rookie card. This 1996 issue of Kobe Bryant was available before he became a Lakers star. However, many collectors insist that rookie cards must show players in NBA uniforms. (Copyright © Pacific Trading Cards, Inc.)

Remember, the "rookie" label doesn't apply only to cards of players. If a coach who's never played in the NBA gets his first job in the league, his first card will carry the "rookie" designation, too.

PAST PLAYERS, PRESENT VALUES

Once players call it quits, some of their cards can keep gaining in value. The hobby can decide that certain sets are harder to find than once imagined. Or, when a player gains a post-basketball career that's just as unique, the price of his cards will only benefit.

Take the case of Bill Bradley of the New York Knicks. His card values climbed when he retired at the end of a fine career. They climbed again when he was elected a U.S. senator, and even more when he was chosen to the Basketball Hall of Fame. When Bradley retired from the Senate and wrote a best-selling autobiography, that helped his card prices, too. Rumors followed that he would run for president, giving collectors another reason to pay more for his cards.

The Hall of Fame gives permanent appeal to cards of all its members, not just Bradley's. The Hall, located in Springfield, Massachusetts, has been in existence since 1968. Every May, new members are welcomed in a special ceremony. The Hall has more than 200 members. The rules require that players and coaches be retired at least five years before getting elected. Some card dealers keep track of basketball retirees who are likely to be voted into the Basketball Hall each year, and the card values start inching up even before the votes are counted. Even the most expensive cards will jump in price from 10 to 25 percent once a retired star makes the Hall.

ESPN announcer Dan Patrick starred on his own subset for 1996–97 Upper Deck. Surprisingly, star and rookie players weren't identified on card-front photos. (Copyright © the Upper Deck Company)

Boston star Reggie Lewis died unexpectedly from heart problems on July 27, 1993, at the height of his career. An unrealized star, his cards gained value shortly after his shocking death. Today, most of his cards sell at common prices again. (Copyright © the Upper Deck Company)

PLAYERS AND VALUES REBOUND!

Another, newer Bradley offers a different example. As a 7-foot 6-inch rookie, Shawn Bradley was considered a "can't miss" choice by many hobby predictors. He was famous for more than his size: Bradley put off basketball for a year in order to serve his church. But later with the Philadelphia 76ers, then with the New Jersey Nets, Bradley looked more like a journeyman player than a great one. He was lumped into a multiplayer trade to the Dallas Mavericks for the 1997–98 season.

Prior to this time, Bradley's cards moved from hotly traded investments to commons. But after the trade, his career seemed to rebound in preseason games. Bradley was grabbing rebounds and blocking shots like never before. Some hopeful hobbyists started stashing away Bradley cards, now quite cheap, anticipating a miracle. But when Dallas won only two of its first 14 games and the coach was fired, Bradley's underdog star dimmed. The moral is that card prices of anyone can move up and down weekly, like stock-market prices—or a yo-yo.

SHOOT FOR THE STARS

At every card shop and card show, take every chance to search the commons piles, new and old. If you have an up-to-date education about

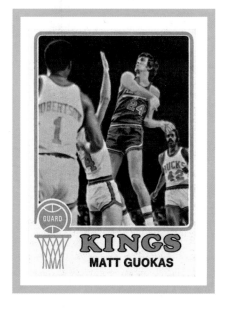

This 1973–74 Topps card gained new appeal long after Matt Guokas retired. He became known as an NBC-TV announcer. Even better, Hall of Famer Oscar "Big O" Robertson is also seen in the card. (Copyright © Topps Company, Inc.)

COLONELS
MIKE GALE

current players and upcoming rookies, you might find tomorrow's valuable cards today, at incredibly cheap prices. Maybe the dealer hasn't read about the career rebound of an experienced player. Maybe the dealer doesn't have your hopeful outlook for a young player's future and wants to sell those cards at any price. After all, some dealers feel that some profit is better than no profit. They'll go against the declared values of basketball-card price guides, just to make sure they make some money.

Finally, regional interest and time of year will confuse the card categories. Hang around the Houston area, and hobbyists may insist that most of the Rockets are stars or semistars. Or wait until the NBA season is over. Cards of *all* the members of a championship team may be more popular (and expensive!), especially if overlooked players helped the team in postseason play. If a little-known player led the league in an overlooked department like steals or assists, some card-holders might say that the numbers prove the guy is going to be a star. When the next season starts, though, all the top card names could change again.

What doesn't change are your chances of getting a star or a rookie or Joe Nobody when you open a new pack of cards. Card companies usually print the same number of all standard cards (not including inserts). Star or rookie cards just seem harder to find because more people want them—and keep them. Companies simply print the cards. Only collectors make the rules about which cards are the most valuable. As a collector, you're more than a player—you're a referee, too. Only you can make the call of what you want to collect.

PASS OR FAIL? CARDS MAKE THE GRADE

Each basketball game begins with a tip-off. The way to tip off a successful career as a basketball-card collector is to know the basics.

The world of basketball sometimes has little to do with the world of cards. When it comes to determining how much money a card is worth, for example, condition matters more than the name and face on the card front. A Larry Bird card in poor condition shouldn't bring any more money, or interest, than a shredded card of any no-name NBA drifter.

All cards get graded by hobbyists, no matter how new or old the cards, no matter how famous the faces. Card conditions, with their common abbreviations, include:

MINT (MT)

A mint card has no problems, large or small. In fact, the word "mint" means new, or just made. A mint card has four sharp corners, a well-centered picture with borders equal on all sides, and with all edges intact. The card still has a shine, with no scratches from handling or fading from being in too much light. Likewise, a mint card is free from all printing problems, such as ink blobs or out-of-focus images.

NEAR MINT-MINT (NRMT-MT)

Think of "mint" and "near mint-mint" as the difference between an "A+" and an "A," with only one tiny problem found on the card. Reasons to downgrade a card to NRMT-MT include tiny printing defects in the ink or photo, or a small nick on only one corner. Note that the borders must remain nearly centered, with edges and color intact.

NEAR MINT (NRMT)

In school terms, this would be an "A-" instead of an "A." This card would have one minor flaw, easier to spot. To fall to NRMT, a card might have one corner that has lost most of its point or all corners might have a bit of wear. The image on the card front doesn't seem as centered. One or two card sides might have been scraped. Printing quality may be less than perfect. However, the card surfaces are still bright and shiny.

EXCELLENT-MINT (EXMT)

How about a "B+"? All but one card corner may be worn. The card image has shifted even more off-center. Expert graders allow only two of the following defects: slightly rough edges, minor color fading, and slight printing defects. A glossy surface remains, though.

EXCELLENT (EX)

Teachers would say an EX card rates a "B." None of the corners of this card have survived without wear. The image is off-center, almost leaning to one side of the card. The edges may be worn, with imperfect printing, fading, and a loss of shine.

VERY GOOD (VG)

Consider this a "B-" or a "C+." While a card like this may not have been tortured, it hasn't been given a hobbyist's protection, either. The card corners are wearing away, as the layers of cardboard start to separate. The edges may seem jagged, and the surface is less glossy and colorful, yet smooth. Only the lightest

Die-cut technology means that cards can come in any shape. The shape of the numeral "1" doesn't refer to Vaughn's fame or jersey number, but his status as a first-round draft pick. With extra corners to crease, die-cut cards can be harder to keep in mint condition. (Copyright © The Score Board, Inc.)

creases, which may look like folds, are allowed for a VG grade. Some hobbyists consider this grade of card unworthy. Others consider these cards as the lowest passing grade they would collect.

GOOD (G), FAIR (F), POOR (P)

The grades start getting scarier here. G, F, and P hobby grades might match a "C-," "D," and "F" in class. The grade depends on how injured the card looks. These cards have differing degrees of major damage. Creases large and small may be found, and all four corners may have varying kinds of wear. Card fronts are scuffed, with little gloss remaining. Some even have handwriting from the card's former owner! In the old days of the hobby—before traded/update sets were produced—young fans would edit their own cards. They'd grab a ballpoint pen, scribble out the player's former team, and note his new club.

Those early collectors didn't know any better. The early days of card collecting had other problems, too. Before specially designed cardboard storage boxes were available, younger, cash-strapped collectors would let cards bounce about loosely in shoe boxes. Cards might even be bundled tight with rubber bands. The rubber bands would carve grooves in the cards, or discolor the cards due to chemical preservatives.

Cards in poor condition have been abused in various ways. Perhaps they were carried in back pockets, instead of in plastic protective pages. Older collectors may remember using clothespins to fasten extra cards to bike spokes, in order to produce a motorcycle sound!

HOW CARDS SUFFER

Basketball cards can have hard lives. Just look at the checklist of possible condition problems compiled by the *Beckett Basketball Card Monthly* magazine:

bubbles in surface
diamond cutting
  (slanted borders)
scratched-off cartoon or puzzle
scratches
chemical or sun fading
erasure marks
miscutting
bleached or retouched borders
water or coffee stains and
  writing, such as adding the
  collector's name to the card
tears

gum and wax stains
notching
off-centered back
rubber-band marks
mildew
surface impressions
  and warping
holes
tape marks
trimming
defective or off-center
  foil stamping

Problems like these seem fairly easy to spot. But some card problems are trickier, the difference between an "A+" and an "A":

- The kinds of abuse that a card might receive often begin on a card's corners. Once, all four corners were sharp and straight, precise right angles. Card graders give corners five different grades, similar to A – F school grades, to note a corner's five stages of wear. Worn corners can make a card become more circular than square.
- Before "full bleed" photographs, all card photos were framed by four borders. Cards were printed on sheets of 132 and then cut into singles. Collectors would find many cards with poor centering. Fleer's first-ever set in 1961–62 was plagued by poorly cut cards. Collectors found miscuts with half of two different cards sharing one card front! But most often, cards lack part of one or two borders, with the photograph appearing to fall off the card front.
- Creases are folds or tears in the card. The worst creases interrupt the photo on the card front or destroy part of the cardboard.

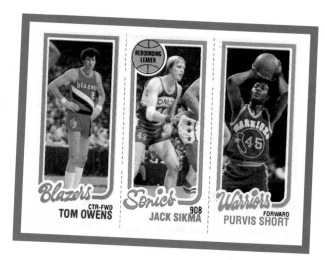

In 1980–81, Topps promised collectors "24 cards in all" in one pack for a quarter. In reality, eight regular-sized cards were each divided into three different single-player panels. Few people tore the cards into three pieces, which would have endangered their condition. By the way, the author isn't related to the Blazer "Tom Owens." (Copyright © Topps Company, Inc.)

SEEING ISN'T BELIEVING

Unfortunately, there is no hobby hospital to make worn cards "like new" again. Some hobby dealers, however, take advantage of this problem, doing their own sneaky doctoring of cards.

For example, if a black-bordered card has a chip or ding, some wrongdoers will cover up the mark with crayon or marker. A tougher trick to catch is the trimmed card. If a border is uneven or worn, the card is shaved to make it appear mint again. Only by using another card from that same set is it possible to discover that the altered card may be one millimeter smaller.

But suppose the wounded card isn't retouched. Is a card in fair-to-good condition worth the bother at all? Many dealers would value a card in poorer condition at no more than 20 percent the amount the same card in mint condition would bring.

Many collectors would say the card is a worthwhile "filler." If you are trying to complete a set, a "filler" card will put you closer to your goal. After you finish the set, you can always look for nicer versions of some cards.

WHOSE CARDS ARE BEST?

Watch out for dealers who play games with hobby grading. Some sellers invent their own terms. "Gem mint" and "mint plus" mean nothing. They are only fancy ways of tricking buyers into paying more for a mint condition card. It's like in school: Teachers may give an "A+," but never an "A+++." Right?

Another problem in judging a card's condition is putting too much faith in the card company. Some dealers might say

Collectors in the 1990s came to expect accents of gold foil and glossy ultraviolet coating on their cards. But, in the future, will such fancier cards lose condition faster? Pictured is a 1997 "Collector's Edge Impulse" card. (Copyright © Collector's Edge of Tennessee, Inc.)

the card is "straight out of the pack" or "from a factory-collated set." The message is that cards never touched by any hobbyist's hands will be in better shape.

Not always! Remember the miscuts from sets such as 1961–62 Fleer? Printing problems at the factory can make some cards look awful. In the 1970s, when cards were packaged with gum, that sugary treat left a stain on any card it touched.

HUMAN HOBBY ERRORS

But, most often, cards untouched by human hands will attract the best grades. In 1991–92, Fleer made a 72-card set for Wheaties. Eight different Wheaties box backs contained 9-card panels. Collectors who tried cutting out each card individually would find that their set could be graded anywhere from VG to EX, no matter how well they tried to cut straight. The only way collectors could guarantee that each card would have all its borders was not to cut the cards at all, but keep the box backs whole.

Another example is any perforated team sheet. At a team's card giveaway game, the cards come in one sheet, with instructions to tear along the lines to make individual cards. Suppose a star card you want is in the middle. Keep the sheet whole, anyway! To some hobby minds, "mint" means in perfect, *original* condition. Sometimes, that means not even opening the package! For example, the Kenner toy company made plastic figures of sports stars, sold with a special card of the athlete. But try selling Kenner Starting Lineup cards out of their package, without the figures. You won't get half the price you would for the whole, sealed package of the card and plastic statue.

Wise people know that beauty is in the eye of the beholder. Your dog may be the ugliest dog in the world, but to you no dog is better. Likewise, in the sports-card hobby condition is in the eye of the beholder. Would you be surprised to learn that most sellers overgrade their cards? That means, "My card is great, so pay me a lot." Of course, buyers want to undergrade, meaning "I want that card cheaper, because. . .it's bad!" It's best to see a card in person, up close, to know its true condition. To get the best viewing of a card, make sure the card is in good light and out of its protective holder, if possible.

A card's condition determines how much it costs. This is most important when you are buying. So decide why you are buying this card in the first place. If you want any card of a superstar like Magic Johnson, just to say your collection includes such players, consider paying less money for a lesser-condition card. You only need to worry about great condition if you plan to sell the card later. But if the card is for you, and not for investment, you can make the rules. Once you have a special card, you'll want to treat it like a part of basketball history. By showing respect for your cards, you're showing respect for the game of basketball.

BONUS OR BOGUS?

In the good old days, a basketball card was just a basketball card. Sure, a few might be double-printed, making extra appearances on each printing sheet of cards. But the basic belief was that a collector had almost the same odds of pulling any card from one pack.

Then companies started developing insert cards, cards that would be randomly inserted only in some packs. In the late 1980s companies called these inserts "chase" cards. The term was soon dropped, however, perhaps because the word made collectors think of a "wild goose chase."

Topps invented the idea of adding a one-per-pack bonus to help sales of basketball cards. In 1969 and 1970, folded posters were the prize. Fleer brought the insert idea closer to its norm of today when the company resumed making basketball cards in 1986. Fleer's 11-card wax pack, retailing for 50 cents, also gave buyers one card-size player sticker. The front contained a player action photo, and the back a biography. Collectors knew right away that Fleer stickers would be harder to get—after all, only one of every 12 items in a Fleer pack was a sticker.

For its 1990–91 set, Fleer began the current practice of creating additional *cards* as inserts. A 12-card "All-Stars" set was offered. On average, one in every five packs would hold a special card. The same odds were true for "Rookie Sensations," a 10-card set. But the "Rookies" weren't included in wax packs. Collectors had to buy 23-card cello packs to find "Rookie Sensations" cards. The subset cards were numbered "1 of 10" or "8 of 10," to avoid being confused with the 198-card standard set.

In 1991 the insert game quickened. Among the five types of inserts offered in various packs, Fleer included a 12-card set highlighting the career of young Dikembe Mutombo. Approximately 2,000 cards were autographed by Mutombo.

Meanwhile, Upper Deck launched its first basketball set, a 500-card effort. Hall of Famer Jerry West autographed 2,500 inserts sprinkled randomly in those first Upper Deck packs. But the biggest news was made by the company's "Award Winner Holograms." Nine cards saluted the previous season's NBA statistical leaders, using the foil-like hologram technology to make the photos seem alive. No longer were inserts easily confused with "regular" cards. These cards hinted at how companies would soon use every high-tech tool possible to make inserts seem special.

INSERTS GET FANCY

Holograms, die-cuts (cards created in unique shapes), and cards made of leather, canvas, and other materials are recent innovations. In 1997 both Upper Deck and ScoreBoard placed actual pieces of game-worn player jerseys on insert cards. The Collector's Edge Impulse set even

Fleer placed one sticker with 12 cards in a pack for the 1988–89 set. Fleer made 11 stickers in all, creating a forerunner of today's insert cards. Most of the stickers came stained on their backs, where glue from the wax wrapper leaked. (Copyright © Fleer/SkyBox Corp.)

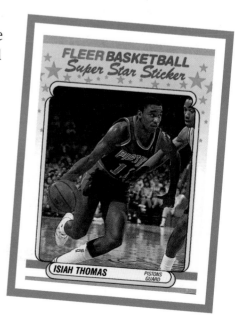

Technology allows cardmakers to make eye-popping inserts. The 1996 "JumpBall Hoop-Cel" insert looked like stained glass. The see-through illusion made players seem to burst through a basketball net. (Copyright © Pacific Trading Cards, Inc.)

offered pieces of game-used NBA balls on inserts.

How special are these additions and innovations? Wrappers may list insert set names, with a notation like "1:24." Read closely. Some new hobbyists wrongly believe that one of every 24 cards *will* be an insert. But the odds actually state that you *might* get one insert in every 24 *packs* that you open.

THE EASY INSERTS

Other inserts aren't that hard to find. In fact, they're the same cards you find in the basic set, with just a small change or twist. Maybe the insert card of Joe Guard looks like his regular card, except the border is gold. Or his insert card features a reproduction of his autograph. "Toppsgold" and the Upper Deck "silver and gold signatures" are common examples of such variations. This kind of insert is sometimes called a "parallel set."

The extreme for a parallel card is the "refractor." Topps promoted this idea in its "Finest" and "Bowman's Best" sets. Refractor cards seem identical to their regular set counterparts. However, tilt them in the light, and they "refract" a rainbow of colors. Because the cards were hard to identify without seeing them sparkle, the company started including an "R-" prefix in front of each card number, to distinguish a refractor.

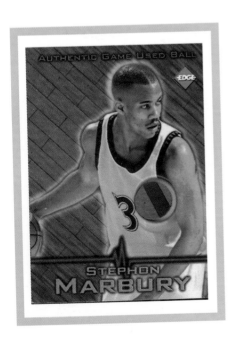

If collectors couldn't get a hand in a game, they could at least get a piece of a game-used NBA ball embedded in a card. The odds of finding one of these awesome inserts was listed at one per 36 packs. (Copyright © Collector's Edge of Tennessee, Inc.)

Pacific Collection's 1996 gold-embossed Draft Picks issue of 54 cards included two parallel sets. Metallic Silver cards averaged one appearance per 13 packs, while Presidential Platinum (pictured here) averaged one per 721 packs. (Copyright © Pacific Trading Cards, Inc.)

Many current inserts feature separate, sequential numbering. If only 500 of a certain card are being produced, the card might read "250 of 500." This does not mean that 500 different players are featured in that set of inserts. Instead, the number indicates that there are 500 cards like yours, and yours was made in the middle of the print run.

AUTOGRAPHED EXTRAS

Fleer/Skybox, in its 1996–97 offerings, developed "Autographics." That year, the company had seven types of packaging for its sets. Autographed cards of 95 different players were randomly inserted in packs of all seven products. The next year's sets offered signatures of 150 different players. The company guaranteed that the cards had authentic autographs—signing sessions were supervised by employees, and even videotaped! To make the cards even more exclusive, only the first 100 cards would be autographed in black ink. The rest would be signed in blue. With a suggested retail of 99 cents for a 10-card pack, Skybox Hoops offered cheap odds for a chance at an "Autographic" insert. But the odds were one in an average of 240 packs! Other brands with similar inserts were more expensive, but had better odds.

Inserts do help sell more packs. For even after a collector has completed a set, there's still

One of Fleer's first insert sets, offered in 1991 packs, used creative paintings by airbrush artist Terry Smith. On average, one in six packs would include a "Pro-Visions" insert. (Copyright © Fleer/SkyBox Corp.)

The 1994–95 Upper Deck Collector's Choice created two parallel sets. These were standard cards from the set with only minor variations. One "silver signature" card, found in every pack, added a silver facsimile autograph to the basic card. "Gold signature" cards would be found in about one of 35 packs. (Copyright © the Upper Deck Company)

a temptation to find a great, rare card. Some stores, such as WalMart, may get exclusive inserts. Only when you get a pack from that store chain do you have a chance at finding a new type of insert.

ADDICTED TO INSERTS

Insert mania has created a type of gambling for collectors. While some collectors wouldn't buy a lottery ticket because their chances aren't good, they'll still open piles of packs. But if you don't want the other cards in the set, don't waste your money on packs. Getting that one popular insert can be as unlikely as hitting a lottery's million-dollar jackpot.

Price guides often list new insert cards at high values. When the inserts are still available in packs, collectors think of those special cards every time they open a pack. Collectors find out

The fine print of this wrapper states that the odds listed for finding an insert card did not apply to the odds per box, but to the odds of finding an insert card among all the packs that were made. Some boxes might produce lots of special cards, while other boxes held few. (Copyright © Fleer/SkyBox Corp.)

Collectors had a one-in-three chance of finding an "Upper Deck SP Championship Shots" insert in a 1995–96 pack, with 20 insert cards in the set. Even popping 60 packs wouldn't guarantee an insert set. After all, "odds" are only an estimate. (Copyright © the Upper Deck Company)

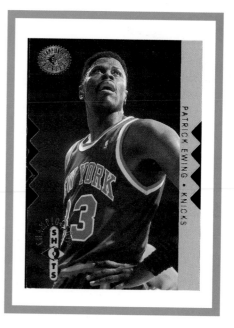

how hard it is to find an insert in a pack, and may choose to buy just that one card from a dealer instead of spending more money on packs. But don't think hard-to-find insert cards are always climbing in price. After seeing how expensive a new insert becomes, some dealers will start opening hundreds of packs. More insert cards appear in hobby shops. Collectors start to wonder how rare those cards really are, and demand—and price—could quickly drop.

Furthermore, new basketball inserts seem to come every couple of months. Your past inserts may quickly become old news. When inserts are no longer current, the demand and price could dip again. Additionally, inserts keep a name value. If players shown leave the game or lose skills, fewer people may want their cards.

That's why you might want to consider how long you'll want to keep your insert. Cashing it in while price and appeal remain high could get you more hobby spending money. Sure, the insert could keep rising in value, but there's no guarantee. Of course, if you had the experience of opening the pack in the hobby shop, pulling that choice autographed insert, and having the whole store cheer for you, keep your prize. That memory may be worth more than any price-guide listing.

"Talkin' Hoops" was a 30-card insert for the 1997–98 Hoops set. One insert came in every first-series pack, offering comments from Hall of Famer-turned-announcer Bill Walton. (Copyright © Fleer/ SkyBox Corp.)

THE HOME-COURT ADVANTAGE

Basketball teams love to have the home-court advantage—playing at home on a familiar court, in front of friendly faces.

Collectors can't find a better home-court advantage than their nearest hobby shop.

There's no need to order by mail or over the Internet if you have a local store that specializes in sports cards. Often called "hobby shops," these places have special shelves and cases filled with basketball cards, old and new, along with other basketball collectibles and hobby supplies.

Why should you bother with a hobby shop when a department store might save you a couple of bucks per month?

Good question. However, think of what you'll get besides cards at the hobby shop.

HOBBY-SHOP SPECIALTIES.

The hobby shop may be run by hobbyists. These employees may be collectors, too. If you buy a hand-sorted complete set of Topps Stadium Club, you can bet that each card was examined before it went into the box. On the other hand, if you purchase a factory-collated set offered at a department store, the store may not understand your problem about one missing card, or several miscut cards. They're only selling what the card-maker sent.

Here's another often-told story around hobby shops. The toy store in the mall offers the same packs for a dime less. Well, customers can't come back to that toy store and ask to buy the remaining four cards they need to complete a set. At the hobby shop, customers who buy a box of packs have help waiting. Did you get enough cards to make a set? If not, the hobby store should have a pile of common cards you can sort through, buying only cards you need.

Can you imagine telling a department-store worker that you'll only buy the best cards out of the pack? Or asking the chain-store employee to pop a couple of Bowman packs for you, because you only want a card of Jerry Stackhouse? Hobby stores do it all for you—selling the stars, the rookies, or sorted team sets (all of the Chicago Bulls cards from a set, for example).

TWO DIFFERENT WORLDS

In fact, card companies know that choosing between hobby stores and department stores confuses some collectors. That's why makers like Upper Deck now produce separate packs called "hobby only" and "retail only." One kind goes to hobby stores, the other to the chain stores. The companies will even produce different insert cards, only available in packs from one type of seller. Of course, the companies hope that collectors will buy lots of both kinds of packs, increasing profits for everyone.

To give collectors more chances to find more cards, some hobby shops run "bid boards." These are monthly or weekly auctions. Cards owned by the store owners, or brought in by other collectors, are displayed. Customers may see a minimum bid posted (that's the lowest price the card's owner will sell for). If not, bidders can try to buy a card for as little as possible. Of course, you're competing against other people who want the same card for the same bargain price. If you set a dollar limit for yourself, and don't overspend by trying to beat other buyers, you can find some bargains.

BUYING BARGAINS EARLY

Here's another hobby-shop bonus: Ask your hobby store if it would "pre-order" upcoming cards you are interested in. Store owners often will offer boxes of a product, such as the newest Fleer Flair, at a guaranteed price. You'll pay in advance and get the box when it's shipped by a promised delivery date.

This gives the dealer money in advance to obtain a quantity of the cards. Sellers, whether a small shop or a huge chain store, get better prices when they buy more. If the store pays less to get cards from the company, it's often willing to charge you less.

If you pass up a bulk pre-order offer, you may find the dealer is selling packs you could have had for $2 at a $4 rate. Perhaps the company didn't print as many cards as promised, or raised the prices it charged dealers. Maybe every collector wants a certain hot-selling rookie card out of those packs.

A HOBBY CLASSROOM?

A hobby shop is often the place in which collectors, like you, learn about new products or trends. But remember: Hobbyists learn from each other. A shop owner who has been busy collating team sets may not have had a chance to read about the new rookie sensation. Owners can learn from collectors like you. So don't complain that the hobby store doesn't get the "hot" basketball cards if you haven't told the store owner what you're wanting! Furthermore, few stores have the time, space, or money to carry every new trading card made. Most store owners try to sell cards from all sports, to appeal to as many customers as possible.

Most stores don't buy from—or swap with—customers, either. That's because hobby stores, like big department stores, need to make money. Workers need to be paid. New cards and products have to be bought from companies. And stores have to pay rent. Did you know that stores in some malls even have to pay part of their profits to the building owners?

That's why a dealer probably won't pay the price-guide amount for your card. After all, when the dealer resells the card, who would pay more than price guide? And if dealers only made back the same money they pay out, there's no profit for rent and workers. The same hard facts affect dealers in trading. If you want to trade for a $10 Jason Kidd card, you might be asked to offer $20 worth of cards in return. Profits have to come first.

HOBBY-SHOP SURPRISES

Yet shop owners will share deals whenever possible to please their regular customers. In 1997 hobby shops passed out postcards from Topps. The company wanted to know, "Why do you collect?" Anyone who sent in an answer got a free pack of Stadium Club basketball cards and an issue of *Sports Cards* magazine as thanks. More than 15,000 hobby-shop customers cashed in on that deal.

But maybe the best part about being in a hobby shop isn't that you can surround yourself with basketball cards. The best part comes from being around so many other people who love basketball cards as much as you do. That's why some customers will stand at the counter, opening packs on the spot. Chances are that the store workers know your favorite team and player, and will cheer when you pull out an insert or hot card.

Hobby shops are excellent places in which to acquire basketball cards and hobby knowledge. Even if you aren't buying, look and listen. Each visit is a free education, a news broadcast of what hoops collectors in the area can expect from the coming season.

ROAD GAMES

Basketball-card dealers have collections of cards. Card shows have collections of basketball-card dealers.

There they are, all under one roof, like a mall full of nothing but hobby shops. Dealers come together for a show, bringing some of their best items, each manning tables filled with their various cards and collectibles. If the first table you stop at doesn't have that Kobe Bryant card you want, move on. Or if that first dealer wants too much money for the card, see if a seller down the line is willing to listen to offers.

That's right, you can sometimes make a deal. Although show dealers have to pay for their trip to the show, including food, gas, and maybe an overnight stay in a hotel, many don't have other ongoing expenses. Some card-show dealers do have shops back home. But others just run mail-order businesses. A one-time rental fee for a space at the show is their main cost. If dealers are spending less money on their business, they might not mind making less profit.

A card show is the place to be for comparing cards and prices. To get the most out of your visit, start by knowing the show. For a smaller event, make sure to call one or two days before. There's nothing sadder than a family who has traveled for hours to attend a canceled event, the show that never was.

Are the biggest shows the best shows? Not always. The few tables set up at a shopping mall or flea market could have better prices than the sports collectors' conventions advertised in hobby magazines.

That's because big-show promoters have to pay big appearance fees to induce current players and Hall of Famers to come and sign autographs. To make that money back, promoters charge dealers big fees for table space, and sell admission tickets to collectors. And, to get more collectors to come, promoters spend more money on advertisements.

Meanwhile, the local show of a few tables could feature "weekend warriors." These dealers are part-timers who have regular, non-hobby jobs. They come to small shows simply to earn money, not for food and clothes, but to build their own collections.

When reading advertisements for larger, regional shows, look at the fine print. Along with admission fees, information about corporate sponsors or partners might be listed. If you see the logos for Upper Deck or Fleer or other card manufacturers in an ad, get excited. Often, card companies will set up booths at bigger shows. They'll hold contests, have employees answer questions about new cards, or give away the promotional card samples that collectors crave.

But no matter what size show you want to attend, set your game plan first. Here are some helpful shopping strategies:

TRY TO SHOP FOR BASKETBALL CARDS DURING THE OFF-SEASON

In the summer everyone is talking about baseball. In September the beginning of football may be the popular topic. You might have to look harder for basketball cards on dealer tables at those times. But when you find them, you may also find that the dealer is anxious to get rid of off-season stuff—and you'll get a better price.

This rule doesn't always help—for example, with value-climbing prices for top rookies, or high-demand cards of legends like Michael Jordan. Yet when the whole world is talking about a close race in the NBA playoffs, some dealers might think that every card picturing players from those teams should sell for extra. Prices are often better in the off-season.

KNOW THE LAY OF THE LAND AND THE TEAMS OF THE LAND

While Jeff Hornacek was beefing up the Utah Jazz teams in the late 1990s, his cards were gaining value in an odd place. Hobby shows in central Iowa saw lots of interest in Hornacek cards. That's because he'd been a star player for Iowa State University years before.

Of course, Hornacek's cards could be hiked in value by Utah dealers, promoting their new local hero. Shoppers at shows in either region would need to understand the interest in those individual cards, and be willing to pay extra.

But hobbyists in southern or eastern states might find cards of Hornacek or other Jazz players to be plentiful—and cheaper, too!

THE MIDDLE COMES LAST

Hobby history shows that the best prices and deals come in the opening, or closing, hours of an event.

For instance, if Grant Hill is signing autographs at your neighborhood card show, expect dealers to want more than the going price-guide value for his cards minutes before the signing. At the end of the day, after the star has left the building, some dealers might discover that all the show attendees brought their own cards for autographs. These leftover cards might now be sold at reduced prices.

Dealers often have two mind-sets. First, they may want to make as much money as fast as possible, to pay table rental and travel expenses. Other dealers might be stingy until the final moments of the show. Then, realizing that their sales figures were disappointing, they'll chose to give you a deal. That way, they'll have some money to show for their work—and have a lighter load to carry home.

FEEL THE DEAL

Asking a dealer to sell an item for less money might seem harder than slam-dunking over Shaquille O'Neal. Just remember, anything's possible—though some ground rules can help your odds!

- It's best to go one-on-one with a dealer. Time your drive. Asking the dealer to sell you a two-dollar card for a buck in the middle of a crowd of collectors can bring doom. Most dealers will say no, knowing that everyone else listening will crow, "Hey! Sell to me at half-price, too!"

- Go for the three. Three-pointers don't always work, but they bring big scores when you're on the mark. A three-step negotiation can work, too. Imagine this matchup:

Dealer: That Kevin Garnett card books at three bucks.
Kid Collector: How about a dollar?
Dealer: I need at least two dollars.
Kid Collector: Sold!

Do the math. See how the card was priced three times, with the price changed by one-third? A price reduction of 25 percent (taking a quarter off for every dollar) is common. A 33 per-

This 1993 Classic Draft Picks card looks, on one side, like a regular card from that year's set. But the flip side shows that this special freebie was available only to folks attending the 1993 National Sports Collectors Convention. This promo was available for just three days. (Copyright © The Score Board, Inc.)

cent reduction (of $3 to $2) is possible. Getting a half-price markdown can be done, although your chances there are like those last-chance buzzer shots from deep three-point land . . . iffy, if at all.

Note that most dealers will laugh (or swear!) and stomp away when someone asks for more than half off a card. For instance, if a price guide claims that new Allen Iverson insert card should sell for $10, you might make your case with a $5 offer. Offer only $2, and you'll probably get a nasty response from the other side of the table. A common dealer response to such "low-ball" offers sounds something like this: "If you think my cards are so worthless, why are you wasting your time and mine?"

Furthermore, don't try to fib, saying, "The dealer over there sells it cheaper." The likely dealer reply will be, "Fine. Buy it there." Dealers scout their competition. They know their prices have to be at or below other prices in the room. Worse yet, collectors who try to make dealers oppose each other for lowest prices may get shunned by every seller. Believe it or not, many dealers are friends who stick together.

BRING READING MATERIAL

Do you have a recent price-guide magazine? Be sure to bring it to the next show you attend. It's like having another person beside you to help negotiate your purchase.

These days, most dealers won't bother putting prices on many single cards. Instead, they'll flip open their "Beckett" and tell you how much the magazine estimates those cards are worth. Still, have a magazine of your own. If a dealer is sure the card you want should cost five bucks, instead of the dollar the price guide claims, politely point out the difference. It's fine to say, "I was hoping to get the card for book value." Some dealers might agree to meet the price. Others may explain why they want more. Maybe they themselves paid the Beckett price, expecting the card to become a hot property in the future. Even if you decide not to buy the card, you'll still get a free education about future hobby trends.

Many dealers seem to see nothing wrong with giving you unbagged, unprotected cards, endangering their mint conditions. But dealers have some gripes about young customers, too.

Dealers catch collectors pulling commons, once in numerical order, out of huge piles. Suddenly, the hobbyist doesn't want to buy all the cards. Not only does the dealer make no money, but he has to ignore other customers while resorting and refiling the unwanted cards in their order by number. Some dealers stop carrying commons because they take too much time and make too little money.

Here's an easy solution for both the collector and dealer. Bring a handful of index cards with you to shop. Before you look over commons, show the dealer that you'll mark the places of the cards you want in the box. "I'll keep them in order by number this way. Okay?" Watch the dealer's face shine. Maybe your thoughtfulness will even get you a better deal for less money.

LOOK FOR WHAT ISN'T THERE

Suppose you attend a show in the state of Washington. All the dealers are selling SuperSonics cards they have sorted from their commons piles.

"Pardon me, but would you have any other Sonics cards?" isn't a great question to ask. Dealers might think that you mean cards from the nationally issued sets like Upper Deck, cards found in price-guide magazines. You could find those easily anytime, and often at a better price.

Try asking, "Do you have any regional Sonics cards?" The dealer might have thought that people at a Seattle show would already have cards issued so close by. Or the lack of price-guide information might fool dealers into thinking that no one wants the cards.

Be patient and specific in shopping at shows. Some dealers might have the best and cheapest cards hidden under the table. Unless you ask the right questions, you may never see them.

DON'T MISS THE LIST

Surprisingly, few collectors will bring a list of their wants to a hobby show. Some shoppers might insist that they know what they need or like without writing it down. Others think that the fun of a hobby show is buying the first new cards they see.

These mind-sets may cause a few problems.

Suppose the box of Fleer Flair packs you opened left you short of a set by just seven cards. Unless you memorize the card numbers you need, you might blow your chance to complete the run of cards for a low price.

Don't get fooled by a big "sale" sign or fancy table display. Don't bite—or buy!—when a dealer says, "That's my last one. They're selling fast." Was the card on your list to begin with? Are you being competitive, trying to buy something just so other collectors won't get it?

Most important, your list helps you make a budget. Use hobby magazines and price guides to estimate the going rates of the cards you want. Write down the amount that you are willing and able to spend for each item. Having it in writing will help you to tell a dealer, "I wanted that Hoops set but can't pay more than $12 for it." These steps will help increase your chances of leaving the show with the cards you need and, maybe, a few bucks to spare.

TALK TO STRANGERS

Dealers aren't the only people to speak with at a show. Other customers can help you save both time and money. If you're at a show that has 50 dealer tables, shopping the whole area for the best price on a new Topps pack might take all day. So if you see someone popping Topps packs in the hotel lobby outside the showroom, ask for advice. "Excuse me, please. Do you remember which dealer you bought those cards from? Could I ask how much they were?" Sometimes, such chats lead to free trading among show attendees.

Best of all, you could make a friendship that will last beyond the end of the day's hobby show.

THE BIGGEST ARENA

Most hoops followers would love to have season tickets to see their favorite team for every game. And most hobbyists would love to go to shows every weekend, or live next door to a huge hobby store. But most of us have limited time and money to spend on the game we love. Lucky for us, there are easier ways to keep informed on new happenings in the hobby and basketball worlds.

Your first stop should be the Internet. With Internet-ready computers available in many homes, schools, and libraries, young collectors have more ways to get more information than ever before.

Once, hobbyists had to wait for monthly magazines, or the weekly *Sports Collectors Digest*, to get news about new sets of basketball cards. Now these hobby media are among the last to share news about new cards.

GETTING NEWS NOW

Card companies give instant reports about new cards to collectors of any age. All you have to do is call up a company's Web page. Under "news releases" are the same stories about new sets that are sent to all the hobby magazines. In fact, you might see almost the same story printed in hobby magazines several weeks later.

The best card companies provide interactive pages, with places for collector feedback. At www.hasbrotoys.com, for example, that company has a special collectors' Web page for Kenner Starting Lineup fans. Hasbro had started including women in some of its Starting Lineup series, such as gymnasts and track stars, but the basketball sets remained a male-only group through 1997.

A spot was available to click on for comments and questions about the athletic figures. At the end of the first Women's NBA season in 1997, a fan sent two questions: Had Rebecca Lobo been included in a set? Would Kenner be making figures of WNBA players?

Even on a Sunday, in less than eight hours, the questions got a detailed response from Jack Farrah, a designer of the sports figures. Despite hobby rumors that Lobo would be featured, the Kenner designer said that problems in production had caused Lobo to be postponed. And, Farrah added, Kenner had no plans at the time to make a set of WNBA figures.

NETTING TEAMS ON THE NET

Well, sure, you might say. Hobby magazines or collectibles companies would try to be helpful on the Internet, in order to get you to buy more stuff. But would team and league Web sites care about the wishes of only one collector? Some yes, some no. The Internet can show you which teams are hobby-friendly. You can check out the upcoming schedules of pro and college teams on-line. Those schedules may list promotional giveaways, giving you an idea of which teams try to reward their fans.

And if the information you want isn't listed, ask for it. The Internet is an equal-opportunity medium. Your message, sent by electronic mail, often gets instant attention. As long as your spelling and grammar are top-notch, there is no clue that you are a kid. You are judged by your message, or your request.

Hobbyists can learn a lot on-line, and swap a lot of information. However, other hobby business goes on daily from computer to computer. Shops, dealers, and individual collectors either set up their own Web sites, or try to buy, sell, and trade through forums and chat rooms. They'll leave messages about the cards they have or want.

Sadly, some people have been dishonest about trading and selling on the Internet. Look at messages posted on the "Tuff Stuff" or "Beckett" magazine forums, and you're sure to find a subject line like "Bad Trader" or "Ripped Off." The most common story is of two on-line collectors who agree to trade one card each. The first collector was honest, and sent his trade through the mail. But the second trader claimed the card never arrived, and won't send the card that was promised in return. Many such stories involve inserts or rookie cards, with losses of $20 or more. How do you know who is telling the truth?

BAD NEWS TRAVELS FAST

People share their sad stories because they're trying to help others avoid the problems they found. Still, being more choosy about their hobby partners might have avoided their disappointments.

If you spend a couple of dollars more to send by registered mail or United Parcel Service, you'll get a receipt after your package is delivered, written proof that it reached its destination. If you have such information, your postmaster or the Better Business Bureau might be able to help you get the goods that were promised in trade. But, most often, the best defense is a good offense. In other words, check out the person you're dealing with before you send money or trades.

Collectors of any age should talk by telephone or mail a regular letter to get more information from new hobby people they have met on the Internet. It's a good idea to ask for names of people that your new acquaintance has done busi-

Tsou Hai-Zunkg was part of a 125-card set of the Chinese Basketball Alliance, made by Upper Deck for the 1995–96 season. The cards were sold in 10-card packs, only in Taiwan. The Internet could help you reach collectors who'd have, or want, such cards. (Copyright © the Upper Deck Company)

ness with, and call or write to them, too. Dealers who won't give you names of other people they've done hobby business with aren't worth your time. It's your money and your cards.

Don't be shy about asking for opinions from teachers or other adults who've been around the Internet before. They can help you judge if the sales pitches or trade offers sound fair and honest. We all need to be reminded sometimes of the old, wise warning: "If something sounds too good to be true, maybe it is."

INTERNET INTERVIEWS

Hobbyists can learn more about basic collecting on-line, too. See if others will share their collecting experiences, such as: Did they fail to get a complete set after opening a box of packs? Did they get more inserts than the odds on the wrapper promised? By sharing information, all collectors can spend their money more wisely, getting the cards they want most. Many public schools in many countries have their own Web pages. Find a student hoops fan who wants an "e" pen pal, and there's a chance you'll find a collector who would trade cards.

Any time the e-mail address of a team, hobby author, card-maker, or dealer is printed in an article or on a package, keep track of it. That hints that the person or company wants to know what you're thinking. Send your questions and ideas. Don't think: "Why would someone answer me?" Instead, try asking: "Why not?" In basketball or in your hobby, you'll never score unless you take a shot.

NO HARM, NO FOUL?

Many basketball players shiver at the sound of a referee's whistle. What kind of foul just got called? Who did it? What's the penalty?

Don't get fouled in the collecting game. Knowing what to avoid can spare you hobby headaches and declining dollars.

Be aware of many hobby challenges, including:

AUTOGRAPHS

Suppose you've seen that your favorite New York Knick is signing autographs at a huge hobby show. The price for in-person signatures is $25.

Maybe you think you'll save some bucks by just writing to him for a free autograph in care of the team. You've got a great Topps Finest that'll look swell with a signature. As long as you send a self-addressed, stamped envelope, he has to answer. Then your card will be worth $25 more.

A photo alone can't make a card valuable. Although the Bullets were renamed the Washington Wizards, most collectors wouldn't pay extra just for a look at an old uniform. (Copyright © Fleer/SkyBox Corp.)

Are these cards? Collectors weren't sold on the idea of "Tonx." The cardlike rectangles were sold in cardlike packages. Each piece had a punch-out circle meant to be removed and played with. But the "Tonx" attempt to cash in on the 1990s milkcaps craze died along with that fad. (Copyright © The Score Board, Inc.)

Time out! Don't bet on any of the above ideas coming true. Just because a hobby-show promoter says an in-person autograph ticket costs $25, that doesn't prove the value of the signature. The show promoter has to pay the player for time and travel and make his own profit, too. Another promoter could offer the same signer next month for $5. That price doesn't prove the autograph's value, either.

Mailing for autographs has its problems, too. First of all, the player you like may sign for free by mail, or he may not.

Suppose this particular Knick does. That's still no reason to send your best, most expensive card to him for a signature. Current NBA players get more fan mail than ever before. Teams try to get all the mail sorted and delivered, but there's no guarantee that a Knick written to in care of Madison Square Garden will get every single letter. Even if he does, your card could get mashed, smashed, and trashed, making mint condition just a distant memory. The safest route is to send only less-valued duplicates in the mail, in case they don't succeed in their search for a real signature.

Worse still, when your card gets returned, is it autographed? Chances are, not really. Some players are overwhelmed by fan mail. They use a rubber stamp or an autopen machine to make a copy of their autograph. Their real signature may look like the copy, but that doesn't mean the actual athlete ever came close to your card with a pen. The result is a card in poor-to-fair condition, no better than if your little brother laced your card front with spray paint. Hobby purists even insist that an authentic autograph on a card destroys its mint condition.

In other words, you'll never know if an autograph has lasting cash value. The only reason to get an autograph is that it means something to you, that you want to feel a little closer to the athlete you admire. Standing in line for an in-person signature may or may not get you closer: Sure, you'll see his face and hands better than you could from the stands. You might even get to say hello, or ask a question. But chances are just as great (especially if the player is a star) that you'll be rushed through so that others can get a turn, too. The player may be so busy signing that he'll barely look up at your face. Sometimes, the only way you'll know what a signing will be like is to go there yourself and see.

ONE-OF-A-KIND CARDS

Suppose a friend says to you, "I have a Dennis Rodman card that you don't have. It's a one-of-a-kind error. No price guides list it. No one's seen it."

Your friend flashes a Fleer Rodman where his tattoos don't show up! "All your cards show his tattoos. This one doesn't," he says. Could he really have made a rare hobby discovery?

If something seems too good to be true, maybe it's not true. You can check such mysteries yourself, if you know how. In this case, find some other Fleer Rodman cards from the same year's set. If they showed Rodman's tattoos, your friend could report the error to a hobby magazine and get it confirmed.

But, in this case, you'd find that Fleer and a few other companies didn't want photos showing tattoos on Rodman or any other players in the 1990s. All Rodman's Fleer cards were airbrushed to remove his tattoos. There was no printing error.

In short, even if your best friend believes something is true, it never hurts to check it out.

These 1990–91 Fleer cards frustrated some collectors through their odd looks and unlimited supply. With tiny photo spaces, most cards from this set became unwanted commons. (Copyright © Fleer/SkyBox Corp.)

Fans of Kevin Johnson might find this 1992–93 SkyBox "Team Tickets" card in commons boxes. Why? This strange series didn't identify any players pictured! (Copyright © Fleer/SkyBox Corp.)

THE NEVER-WAS CARD

When adding extra-special, high-priced singles to a collection, most hobbyists worry about buying counterfeit cards. But phantom cards are a more common problem, perhaps an even bigger one. Phantom cards are items not licensed by the NBA or the Players' Association. They might picture a player on a college or high school team. Perhaps only a simple color photo graces the cards.

But if a card is not in any price guide, if it's never been written up in a hobby magazine, think twice. Such cards are often made by someone who got a photo or an old picture and decided to print off some cards, thinking anything with a star's face will sell.

The shady seller might claim that the card was only available in one city, or that it was a "warehouse find." This popular myth tells how the printer ran out of money and couldn't ship the cards to dealers. Years later, this lucky dealer found these undiscovered cards collecting dust. At least, that's how the story goes.

One clue to an illegally made card is that the back might be blank. Only one side of the card was printed to save time and money, to get the bogus product out on the street as soon as possible. Phantom cards aren't worth your money.

The 1994–95 NBA Hoops set printed trivia questions on the backs of these cards. Curious collectors had to look up other cards in the set for answers. Many didn't bother. (Copyright © Fleer/SkyBox Corp.)

To peel or not to peel? Cards like the 1996–97 Topps Finest come with a protective plastic film that can be removed. However, price guides say cards left untouched will be worth more. On the other hand, it's hard to appreciate how exciting the card is all covered with "peel and remove" directions. (Copyright © Topps Company, Inc.)

REPACKAGED ASSORTMENTS

Visit most department stores, and you're sure to find these glitzy card packages. Maybe the box is a collection of unopened packs, or maybe it's a grouping of singles.

Suppose you see a promise that so many inserts will be found in the repackaged package. You see at least one superstar's face. Don't get fooled by a vague term like "insert." Some inserts will be one per pack! Is that so special? Likewise, some repackages have said "out-of-print cards" or "five-year assortment." But the age of a card doesn't promise value. Collectors don't start paying sky-high prices as soon as a card turns one year old!

Another popular line on repackaging is "Price guide value exceeds $200!" or something similar. This could be true. However, what price guide did the company use? More important, what year was that price guide published? As you know, all cards don't go up, or stay up, in value.

Originally costing $1.59 for a 12-card pack, the 1993–94 Fleer Jam Session set made the NBA's big men look even bigger. However, the 240-card set wouldn't fit in the standard nine-pocket sheet, creating a new collecting challenge. (Copyright © Fleer/SkyBox Corp.)

TV SHOPPING

It's unlikely that a dealer will chase you down the street for five minutes, begging and bullying you to buy a card set. But some dealers invade a collector's own home!

Numerous TV shopping networks have appeared on the television sets of unsuspecting collectors, using basketball stars to help them sell their deals.

Shoppers are blinded by hoop heroes who sit with a sales-host. In between words, the athlete nods and smiles at the next card item up for sale. Sure enough, the huge price that flashes on the screen is reduced! A lower price has been offered. Yet, interestingly, the TV price often soars high above any price-guide figure.

To make the sales pitch more tempting, buyers who call in might get the chance to say hello to the basketball great.

If you do watch a collectibles segment on a TV shopping network show, watch with a price-guide magazine in your hand. Promise yourself that you won't ask an adult to call in a purchase, just because you like the athlete co-host. Listen to the claims, and see how much more you would be paying for the brief thrill of a possible telephone chat with a celebrity. Even with the cards delivered to your home, chances are the TV prices could be triple the going hobby-shop rates. With the extra you don't spend on overpriced collectibles, you might be able to buy a ticket or two to a real game.

VENDING MACHINES

It's not an evil robot, but the steel box almost calls to you. Amid the machines selling candy bars and drinks, a few outlets have programmed the same devices to sell packs of cards.

The problem here is simple. Have you ever been peeved when a vending machine drops your chocolate, cream-filled snack from the top shelf, squishing it before you can catch it? Why should those cards come out of the machine any more gently? Mint-condition cards have never been squeezed and folded between metal prongs, or crunched their corners taking high dives off vending-machine shelves.

HOBBY GRAB BAGS

The paper bag at the hobby show contains 25 cards for five dollars. "Every bag contains a Jordan" or "Rookie cards inside each bag" could be the tempting offers.

Collectors of all ages have hoped and wished that grab-bag gambles held lucky rewards inside. But would you plunk down money, close your eyes, then pick your purchase from a deck, sight unseen? In many cases, dealers are trying to get rid of unpopular cards with little value. Sure, there may be an appealing card included to tempt you to play. Getting something for nothing might sound good. But the somebody who gets nothing could easily turn out to be you.

HOBBY GAMBLES

Roll the dice to win one of the cards posted on the board. Spin a spinner for a chance at a valuable rookie card. Some collectors think a game of chance is a game of skill. They hope, with repeated tries, that practice will make them perfect.

Not so. The price of each try doesn't matter here. It's not only silly to take chances, it's usually illegal. Kids especially aren't allowed to play slot machines at casinos. When dealers allow young people to do

First, Topps offered slightly higher-priced Stadium Club cards. Then, beginning with this 1993–94 offering, Topps "Finest" became a more pricey choice. A 7-card pack had a suggested retail price of $3.99. Of course, the limited supply meant that packs were resold at higher prices. (Copyright © Topps Company, Inc.)

Collector's Choice cards came in many varieties in 1995. Upper Deck issued a Japanese set, changing only the language on card backs. Along with 10-card packs, collectors in Japan got an order-form card, telling how to get a complete first-series set in a binder. (Copyright © the Upper Deck Company)

the same kind of gambling at a card show, they are probably breaking the law.

If you see one of these operations at a card show or shop, tell a parent or adult that you think a dealer is running an illegal gambling operation. If a police officer is near, tell him or her. Don't bother telling adult dealers they are wrong. That's what the law is for.

Think of collecting as if it were a basketball game. Many, if not most, players love the game, respect the rules, and play fair. Likewise, most card sellers and buyers are fans first, people who love basketball and find cards a way to stay closer to the game. Don't think that every collector and dealer you meet in the basketball-card hobby is out to trick you. Most just want to play the game. But playing means making decisions. Pass or shoot? Different choices may bring different rewards, or problems. Knowing—and preparing for—problems before they happen is the best way to keep a winning hobby game plan.

PSST . . . SECRET HOBBY BUYS!

One of the most exciting aspects of a basketball team is the "sixth man," the team's secret weapon. Just when a club needs a boost the most, the super substitute comes off the bench and surprises the other team with new energy.

Sometimes, you may want to have hobby secret weapons, ideas to keep on your own bench. When your money starts to disappear, or when you're simply getting bored or frustrated with one type of basketball card, here are some ideas to give your own collecting game some new energy.

REDEFINE YOUR COLLECTION

So you want to collect basketball cards. Does that mean you should only have piles of little cardboard slabs? Think of all the sidelines you could find to help you showcase the set you're collecting.

Most important is the wrapper or package the cards came in. In the 1990s some hobbyists went wild trying to find surviving wrappers for cards from the 1960s through the 1980s. After all, most collectors threw away the packages after they got what they wanted inside. Because demand for wrappers never seemed

In the beginning, most collectors found cards in wax wrappers. The company would ask collectors to mail in their wrappers for special collectibles. Many wrappers were thrown away. Surviving wrappers from older sets are harder to find than cards, explaining their undiscovered collectibility. (Copyright © Fleer/SkyBox Corp.)

high in the past, the supply of older wrappers has diminished considerably.

One reason wrappers are rare is that companies used to want wrappers returned. Companies still have mail-in offers that promise special card sets or other collectibles, as long as wrappers are mailed in as proof of your product purchase. The few collectors who go to the trouble of answering mail-in offers advertised on basketball-card wrappers are getting true collectibles. In future years, those wrapper redemption prizes may be more valuable than any of the cards found in the packs.

Another reason for rare wrappers: Check at card shops for what you don't see. Is the dealer throwing out empty boxes that housed basketball packs? Did the dealer get posters or shelf displays from the company to advertise the set? Are those display items being used? What will happen to them when the dealer is done with them? Ask about items you might be interested in adding to your own collection. Anything made by the manufacturer of the cards you're collecting should be considered collectible, if the price is right. (And free is a good price, too!)

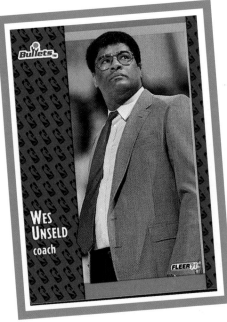

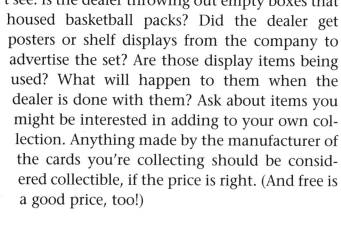

Collectors on a budget don't have to spend big money to get cards of Hall of Famers. Many collectors forget that many coaches began as famous players. (Copyright © Fleer/SkyBoxCorp.)

Upper Deck teamed with Nestlé to make the 40-card "Crunch Time" set, a natural way to promote the company's candy bar. A 99-cent package contained four cards and a small candy bar. The cards saluted players who made important shots in the last seconds of a game. (Copyright © the Upper Deck Company)

DON'T LOOK DOWN ON KID STUFF

Have you asked a police officer if he or she has any cards? Some law-enforcement agencies have printed "safety" sets of NBA and college players. Cards have ideas on their backs about how to stay safe and smart, protecting against drugs, gangs, and other dangers.

Cards have been made to get kids to read more, to get them to study more subjects, and to attend church. Groups like the Fellowship of Christian Athletes have offered printed cards. Card backs have religious messages. Try talking to your teachers, librarians, or youth-group leaders. They may have heard from groups that made such cards.

In all cases, these cards are designed with kids in mind. Even if you don't keep the cards in your own collection, you'll have great trading material. Adults are often too shy to ask for the cards, or fail in getting them from other adults. Adults can only dream of being given cards, free of charge, to collect!

SHOP EVERYWHERE

You think your grocery store doesn't carry cards? Look closer. Food-related cards may appear in every aisle, from cereal boxes and popcorn to hot dogs and bread. Even the candy counter might have cards in disguise. In 1997, Nestlé's Crunch worked with Upper Deck to produce an exciting 40-card set called "Crunch Time." Each card told of how a star player won a big game, with a last-second shot "in the crunch." Each four-card pack, with a suggested retail price of 99 cents, came with a chocolate bar. Special inserts were created, and a wrapper contest was advertised. You could collect everything but the chocolate, but only if you checked the shelves carefully.

One team sticker was inserted in all 1973–74 Topps packs. The Conquistadors played in the American Basketball Association. Many of the stickers were used by young collectors, or thrown away by older hobbyists wanting only cards, making near-mint survivors scarce. Still, the stickers can be found cheaply, due to the lack of players shown. (Copyright © Topps Company, Inc.)

USE THE HOME-COURT ADVANTAGE

Sure, you like the Chicago Bulls best. You would collect only the Chicago Bulls if you could. However, your state university team is being featured on a card set, with a few new cards given away each week at some fast-food places.

Now is not the time to be a basketball snob, or a picky collector. Never forget tomorrow's stars as you're choosing today's cards. Think of how many people would faint over vintage cards from Michael Jordan's days as a North Carolina hopeful. Chances are great that at least one player from every good college team will make it to the NBA. And, as you sit dreaming of NBA cards that are available across the country, you may be ignoring cards that won't be offered in 49 of the 50 states. Talk about cornering the market! Regional cards are available only during the season, for shorter times than national issues. Get regionals while you can, at least as extras to sell or trade.

EXPECT THE UNEXPECTED

How soon do you give up as a collector? If you discover that a team like the Houston Rockets passed out a card set during one game, do you think that only fans lucky enough to have attended that game, or dealers with connections, are going to have those cards?

Hopeful hobbyists find the biggest bargains. If a team has a giveaway, it's worth the price of two stamps to write and ask if any cards remain. Of course, enclose a self-addressed, stamped envelope for a reply. Try to discover the name of a front-office employee (on-line is a good place to look), so your letter won't be answered at random.

Make your request short and sweet. Here's a sample:

```
Dear (team name, or team employee),
        I am (number) years old. I've been a
fan of the (team name) for (number) years.
I always listen to games on radio and TV,
and follow the team in the newspaper.  I've
collected cards for many years, too.
        I'd love to have the cards that are
being given away at the (date) game.  But I
know that getting tickets might be impossi-
ble. Even if I'm not at the game, could I
learn how to obtain one set of the cards for
my collection? I have enclosed a stamped,
self-addressed envelope for your reply.
Thank you!

Sincerely,


(your name)
```

One of the keys to success is to be personal. Writing to a team and sounding like you want every card ever made aren't enough to make your case. Face it, the teams are hoping that those card sets will help sell tickets. Omit your age if you're older than the giveaway age maximum. Some teams will say, "For all fans age 14 and under."

Now consider another hobby "what if." What if you read in your hobby magazines about a Minnesota Timberwolves regional set sponsored by restaurants in the Twin Cities? Do you have to hop a bus to Minnesota for a shot at the cards?

Try the Internet, or find a librarian who can get you a reference book listing company addresses. Find the headquarters of the company—not the team—sponsoring any regional set.

Send a short letter something like this:

```
Dear (fill in company sponsor name),
     I am a (number)-year-old fan of the
(team name), and was happy to learn your
company is sponsoring a set of their cards.
     I'm sorry that none of your businesses
are close to where I live. I'd have no way
to be part of your promotion. Is there any
way I could obtain a set of the cards for
my personal collection?
     I have enclosed a self-addressed,
stamped envelope for your reply. Thank you.


Sincerely,
(your name)
```

Suppose that a place like a SuperValue market or a Taco Bell restaurant is sponsoring the cards. Maybe there's the same franchise in your town, but this store isn't part of the regional card giveaway. Be creative. See if you can talk to the manager of your local franchise. Explain how you are a regular customer and would like help in getting the basketball cards. Maybe that manager is a friend of a manager who runs a store in the area giving cards away.

If not, try sending a cash-register slip or product wrapper to the headquarters when you write for more information. You should offer proof that you patronize that business. Most of all, don't be shy about giving information concerning your shopping and eating habits. Does your whole family like the burgers or groceries that the card-sponsoring company

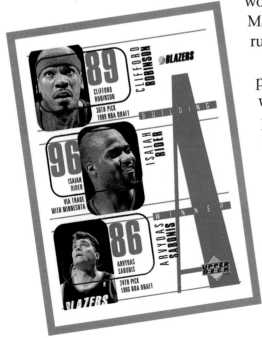

This "Building a Winner" card from the 1996–97 Upper Deck set is termed a "combo" card. Five average players were pictured on front and back, yet it sells at common prices. (Copyright © the Upper Deck Company)

Sometimes a player is seen on many cards in one set. Chris Mullin was depicted on the flip side of the Warriors team checklist in Upper Deck's first-ever 1991–92 set. Collectors would call this a "special" and not Mullin's "regular" card, although it's an inexpensive common. (Copyright © Upper Deck Company)

THE COLLECTOR'S CHOICE ®

sells? Add one sentence that tells how old you are, and how many in your family use those products. Companies know that kids are now choosing the foods and products they'll buy for years to come. Even if you aren't a big spender now, companies hope you'll choose their brands in the future. Maybe sending you some free cards will help you make up your mind, no matter where you live.

LOVE ALL LEAGUES

No, you don't have to watch every basketball game ever shown on television or spend every cent of your savings on game tickets.

Consider the 1997 Pinnacle WNBA cards. When the cards appeared, many collectors still had doubts about the future of women's professional basketball. These doubtful hobbyists didn't realize that this set was a tryout of sorts for Pinnacle, a way to prove that the company deserved the right to make NBA cards. Because the NBA owned the WNBA, the connection was a great one. History-minded hobbyists knew that the "first-ever" basketball sets by Topps and Fleer fetch big bucks. If Pinnacle became a player among future NBA-card makers, this set of women's cards would have extra historic—and cash—value.

The possibilities for basketball buried treasure don't end here. Keep your eyes, ears and mind open, ready to get in the collecting game. Think fast and think of the future.

ALL-STAR IDEAS FOR COMMON CARDS

The fact is, many of the cards you acquire in packs will be "commons," forever seen as low-value, unwanted cards by people not collecting sets. They're called "commons" because they're everywhere.

That's not to say you can't find good uses for commons:

Halloween: Yes, most kids like getting candy for trick-or-treats. However, there's no reason you can't provide a few basketball cards gathered in plastic wrap for each October visitor.

Crafts: Who wouldn't laugh to see their school picture pasted on the body of a slam-dunking Los Angeles Laker? Get out your commons, and try using them to decorate posters, homemade birthday cards, homework assignments, and more.

Garage Sales: Setting up a table at a rummage or tag sale won't bring in lots of collectors willing to pay price-guide rates for rookie cards or inserts. Garage-sale shoppers most often hunt for quantity, not quality.

Offer them bundles of commons, displayed in sandwich bags. Put a player's card from a popular nearby team on top of the pile to shine through the wrapping. Try different sizes of commons bags to sell, 10 cards for a quarter, or 50 for a dollar.

Your Family: Do you have a little brother or sister who always wants to mess with your collection? Instead of screaming for help to keep your star cards from being crushed, use your commons to help your hobby.

Offer a pile of commons to your younger siblings as a present. Explain that they now have their own collection. Tell them you might trade them other cards, if they take care of the first ones they've been given. Spend the money to get them a cardboard storage box, so the cards can be kept safe. You can teach a younger family member about the right ways to collect, while keeping your own cards at a safer distance.

Your Town: Ask teachers at your school if there are any ways that your extra cards could be used in their classrooms. Cards teach geography (where the teams and players are from), mathematics (look at all those statistics!), and writing (some cards seem to tell a player's whole life in 50 words or less).

Next, see if the nearest hospital would welcome your cards. Maybe a teacher, an adult from your church, or an older family member can call for information on how to donate cards for sick kids.

No matter what you decide to do with your extra cards, remember that financial reward is only one benefit your hobby can bring. Sharing your interest with others brings the best, most lasting, reward of all.

A HOBBY FOR EVERYONE

After a half century of play, the National Basketball Association added two new referees for its 1997–1998 season.

Dee Kanter and Violet Palmer joined the officiating staff, giving females their first active roles in the traditionally male-controlled league. Women made hobby history that same year. Pinnacle's 1997 WNBA set was issued one month after the league championship. For the first time, collectors could chase a nationally issued, all-female basketball set. The company issued the cards in sealed tin cans, with 10 cards per container. The suggested retail price was $2.99.

The WNBA ran an on-line store in its first season, helping out card collectors. A 24-can case of the Pinnacle inaugural WNBA cards sold there for $75, only $3 higher than its suggested retail price. That way, collectors around the world would have a chance at the innovative set.

Soon, Fleer was plotting to make a set of cards honoring all-stars from the WNBA's rivals, the women's American Basketball League (ABL). Fleer's cards were made available in conjunction with the ABL's highly touted all-star game at Walt Disney World in the winter of 1998.

Male card dealers weren't always anxious to approve the new cards. Beckett ran its first price listing of the Pinnacle WNBA cards not in *Basketball Card Monthly*, but in *Future Stars* magazine, which deals with minor-league and college athletes. The price guide estimated that the 82-card basic set would bring only $12.50 to $25. Yet even the luckiest collector would need to buy at least nine cans to make a set, costing a minimum of $27. In other words, the magazine's claim of a low set price hinted that collectors were paying too much for a set that few cared about. But the *Future Stars* magazine's brief pricing of the Pinnacle cards is only half the story. For though the set was not considered valuable, the 17 collectible cans—featuring 16 different players and a league logo—were checklisted and priced at $7.50 to $15. Four related WNBA inserts were valued, too.

The rest of the price-guide page was rounded out by mention of the 1996 Topps "USA Women's National Team" 24-card Olympic set, at a price range of $5 to $8. New hobbyists might have been fooled by the price guide into thinking these were the only women's basketball cards ever. But, regionally issued college team sets have been some of the hobby's best-kept secrets.

In 1993–94, the University of Connecticut issued its first women's basketball team set. The set was a perforated 16-card sheet. Rebecca Lobo, who starred in the 1996 Olympics and later became a leading lady with the WNBA's New York Liberty, is the key card in the set. Few dealers have found the cards, and sets have stayed around the $15 level. Surprisingly, when the UConn Huskies women's team went undefeated a year later, the university made no set.

When the first WNBA set was made in 1997, everyone saw stars Lisa Leslie and Rebecca Lobo as "must-have" star cards. As models, commercial spokeswomen, and Olympic stars, they attracted fans and collectors even before the new league's first game. (Copyright © Pinnacle Trading Card Company)

Credit Lobo with introducing the idea of female basket-ballers to a national audience. As card number 82 in Classic Company's Basketball Rookies set, Lobo is the only female among 120 cards. She appeared in assorted Classic sets, wearing a college uniform, in 1995–96.

Classic was the first company to treat female college stars equally. In the 1996 set entitled "Legends of the Final Four," the first 10 cards in the 25-card set were females who starred in the NCAA Tournament. The last five cards featured famed men's and women's coaches. But because the set also features retrospective cards of past players, it has been slow to exceed its $5 to $8 price range. For men's or women's cards, collectors have favored cards of current players in current uniforms.

Listen to California collector Liz Buckman who, at age 23, had been collecting basketball cards for five years. "My younger brothers got me interested in this, and eventually, as they got into other things, I bought their small collections," she says. "I traded and sold cards with children in my neighborhood for two years, and they were all male. They were always happy to come over and see my cards. Me being a woman didn't seem to bother them one bit."

Liz burst onto the national hobby scene by buying a couple of classified "wanted" advertisements in *Sports Collectors Digest*, seeking the Pinnacle WNBA cards. "I usually do not complete sets, but this inaugural WNBA set is very special," she says. "After all these years collecting NBA stars, I can now collect female WNBA stars. I am a huge WNBA fan. I watched every televised game. I'm very happy women are able to play professionally in the United States." Liz noted that cards of Sparks star Lisa Leslie were in high demand in her home state. She used the perfect hobby game plan, finding traders by mail around the country, in places where the supply of some players' cards outweighed the demand.

Looking back at hobby lessons learned, Liz says that card protection might top her list. "I have seen many nice cards ruined because they were not placed in a protector. Kids like to shove cards in their back pockets, or ride bikes while holding their cards in one hand.

"My advice to young girls entering the hobby is to have fun. That's what it's all about—opening a fresh pack of cards and seeing what you get, and making new friends trading cards," she says. "Boys will think you're 'cool' instead of 'just a girl.'"

While Liz says she'd like to see more girls enter the basketball-card hobby, she has advice that could benefit any male or female beginners. "Don't feel pressured into feeling you need high-value, top-dollar cards. All that matters is collecting what you want, keeping the things safe, and sharing your collection with your friends and family."

As Liz waits for more cards of female hoopsters, she maintains a hopeful belief in basketball-card collecting. "The best part of this hobby is that you are free to collect whomever and whatever you want," she says. "There are no mandatory guidelines to follow. Pick your players or teams and get as many items or cards as you can of them."

NBA ADDRESS LIST

Want to get your cards autographed? Want to learn if your favorite team issued its own card set? Be sure to enclose a SASE (self-addressed, stamped envelope) for a reply.

Atlanta Hawks, One CNN Center, Suite 405, Atlanta, GA 30303
Boston Celtics, 151 Merrimac St., Boston, MA 02114
Charlotte Hornets, 100 Hive Drive, Charlotte, NC 28217
Chicago Bulls, United Center, 1901 West Madison St., Chicago, IL 60612
Cleveland Cavaliers, P.O. Box 5000, Richfield, OH 44286-5000
Dallas Mavericks, Reunion Arena, 777 Sports St., Dallas, TX 75207
Denver Nuggets, 1635 Clay St., Denver, CO 80204
Detroit Pistons, Palace of Auburn Hills, Two Championship Drive, Auburn Hills, MI 48057
Golden State Warriors, Oakland Coliseum Arena, Nimitz Freeway and Hegenberger Rd., Oakland, CA 94621
Houston Rockets, P.O. Box 272349, Houston, TX 77277
Indiana Pacers, 300 E. Market St., Indianapolis, IN 46204
Los Angeles Clippers, Los Angeles Sports Arena, 3939 South Figueroa, Los Angeles, CA 90037
Los Angeles Lakers, P.O. Box 10, Inglewood, CA 90306
Miami Heat, One Southeast 3rd Avenue, Miami, FL 33131
Milwaukee Bucks, 1001 N. Fourth St., Milwaukee, WI 53203-1312
Minnesota Timberwolves, 600 First Ave. North, Minneapolis, MN 55403
New Jersey Nets, Brendan Byrne Arena, East Rutherford, NJ 07073
New York Knicks, Two Pennsylvania Plaza, New York, NY 10001

Orlando Magic, P.O. Box 76, Orlando, FL 32802

Philadelphia 76ers, Veterans Stadium, P.O. Box 25040, Philadelphia, PA 19147

Phoenix Suns, P.O. Box 1369, Phoenix, AZ 85001

Portland Trailblazers, One Center Court, Suite 200, Portland, OR 97227

Sacramento Kings, One Sports Parkway, Sacramento, CA 95834

San Antonio Spurs, 100 Montana St., San Antonio, TX 78203

Seattle SuperSonics, Box C-9000911, Seattle, WA 98109-9711

Toronto Raptors, 20 Bay St., Suite 1702, Toronto, Ontario, Canada M5J 2N8

Utah Jazz, 5 Triad Center, Fifth Floor, Salt Lake City, UT 84108

Vancouver Grizzlies, General Motors Place, 802 Griffiths Way, Vancouver, B.C., Canada V6B 6G1

Washington Wizards, U.S. Air Arena, One Harry Truman Drive, Landover, MD 20785

To find any one of the teams on-line, the Internet address is www.nba.com.

HALL OF FAME

Naismith Memorial Basketball Hall of Fame, Box 179, 1150 W. Columbus Ave., Springfield, MA 01101

The Hall of Fame has produced its own cards in the past. Cards or collectibles may be sold by mail. Autographs requests by mail have been forwarded to members. The Hall's Web site is www.hoophall.com.

CONTACT A FORMER PLAYER

To write to a former player who isn't a Hall of Famer, note on your envelope that he's a former player, and send to the player in care of (write: Joe Player c/o) National Basketball Association, Olympic Tower, 645 Fifth Ave., New York, NY 10022. The NBA promises to forward mail. Note "former player" on the envelope.

WNBA ADDRESS LIST

The Women's National Basketball Association teams include:

Charlotte Sting, 2709 Water Ridge Parkway, Suite 400, Charlotte, NC 28217

Cleveland Rockers, Gund Arena, 1 Center Court, Cleveland, OH
    44115
Houston Comets, Two Greenway Plaza, Suite 400, Houston, TX
    77046
Los Angeles Sparks, Great Western Forum, 3900 West Manches-
    ter Blvd., Inglewood, CA 90306
New York Liberty, Two Penn Plaza, New York, NY 10121
Phoenix Mercury, America West Arena, 201 East Jefferson,
    Phoenix, AZ 85004
Sacramento Monarchs, ARCO Arena, One Sports Parkway, Sacra-
    mento, CA 95834
Utah Starzz, Delta Center, 301 West South Temple, Salt Lake
    City, UT 84101
WNBA Headquarters, 645 Fifth Ave., New York, NY 10022
    The league's Web site is www.wnba.com.

WABL ADDRESS LIST

Don't stop searching for pro teams yet. The Women's American
Basketball League can be found on-line at www.abl.com. Their
teams include:

Atlanta Glory, 2100 Powers Ferry Rd., Atlanta, GA 30309
    email: info@atlantaglory.com
Colorado Xplosion, 800 Grant St., Suite 410, Denver, CO 80203
    email: info@xplosion.com
Columbus Quest, 7451 State Route 161, Dublin, OH 43106
    email: alski@columbusquest.com
Long Beach StingRays, One World Trade Center, Suite 202, Long
    Beach, CA 98031-0202
    email: info@lbstingrays.com
New England Blizzard, 179 Allyn St., Suite 403 , Hartford, CT 06103
    email: info@neblizzard.com
Philadelphia Rage, 123 Chestnut St., Fourth Floor, Philadelphia,
    PA 19106
    email: info@phillyrage.com
Portland Power, 439 North Broadway, Portland, OR 97227
    email: info@ableague.com
San Jose Lasers, 1530 Parkmoor Ave., Suite A, San Jose, CA 95128
    email: info@ableague.com
Seattle Reign, 400 Mercer St., Suite 408, Seattle, WA 98109
    email: info@ableague.com

CONTACTING COLLEGE TEAMS

For addresses of the hundreds of college teams that might produce (or star on) regional card sets, one book is the best resource: *The Sports Address Bible: The Comprehensive Directory of Sports Addresses*, compiled by Ed Kobak, Jr. The book is updated every year or two, and contains more than 7,500 listings relating to all types of sports. Ask your nearest librarian to order a copy. Or, for ordering info on the newest edition, contact Global Sports Productions, 1223 Broadway, Suite 102, Santa Monica, CA 90404.

THE OFFICIAL NBA ENCYCLOPEDIA

When you visit the library, check the reference section for one of the most helpful books that any hoops fan or collector could imagine. *The Official NBA Encyclopedia* is just that. The league approves this official collection of history and statistics. The encyclopedia has more than just numbers, however. There are records for every year and for every player and team. This is also the best place to begin learning about the American Basketball Association, the rival league to the NBA from 1967 through 1976.

Buying the book isn't a great idea for budget-minded collectors. The book gets updated statistics every five years. The second edition, from Villard Books, cost $39.95 in 1994. If you want the book only for NBA history, past editions can be found cheaper on bookstore sale tables or used bookshops. Or you can stick to using copies at libraries.

BASKETBALL-CARD COMPANIES

To learn more about basketball-card companies, and their Internet Web site addresses (when available), contact:

Collector's Edge, 2485 West Second Ave. #14, Denver, CO 80223

Fleer/Skybox International, 1120 Route 73, Suite 300, Mount Laurel, NJ 08054
www.skybox.com or www.fleercorp.com

Pacific Trading Cards, 18424 Highway 99, Lynwood, WA 98037
www.pacific-trading-cards.com

Pinnacle/Score, 1845 Woodall Rodgers Freeway, Suite 1300, Dallas, TX 75201
www.pinnacle-brands.com

Press Pass, 14800 Quorum Drive, Suite 420, Dallas, TX 75240

ScoreBoard, Inc. (formerly Classic Games), P.O. Box 1250, Cherry Hill, NJ 08034

Topps/Bowman, One Whitehall St., New York, NY 10004 www.topps.com

Upper Deck, 59099 Sea Otter Place, Carlsbad, CA 92008 www.upperdeck.com

Wheels, 1368 Salisbury Rd., Mocksville, NC 27028

MAGAZINES

To keep track of the whole hobby, including new releases, several magazines are available.

Beckett Basketball Card Monthly, 15850 Dallas Parkway, Dallas, TX 75248

This magazine, which began in 1989, was the first in the hobby to focus solely on basketball cards. The publisher began with a baseball-card magazine, then branched out with new titles for other sports cards.

Even card manufacturers turn to BBCM first when advertising new sets! The magazine is in full-color, except for the famed price-guide center section. The price guide offers the best listings of the tons of different insert cards that appear in packs yearly. Expect most articles to focus on the newest cards and current stars, with only occasional attention paid to cards from the 1970s and before.

Best of all, Beckett samples dealer opinions from various regions of the country each month, relaying comments on different hobby issues. You'll learn about dealer specialties, such as regional card mail-order dealer Steve Taft at Steve Taft Enterprises, 27474 Country Glen Rd., Agoura Hills, CA 91301-3533.

How popular is the *Beckett Basketball Card Monthly*? Beginning in 1997, the price guide and magazine was distributed in Asia in the Chinese language. The first Chinese edition pictured past U.S. covers showing Michael Jordan, including the first-ever Beckett Basketball. (Copyright © Beckett Publications/Taiwan Cardwon Co.)

Tuff Stuff Magazine, P.O. Box 1637, Glen Allen, VA 23060

This monthly reports on all sports cards. It's not the detailed coverage of the *Beckett* monthly, but *Tuff Stuff* is a fun alternative. New basketball card-related collectibles like the Kenner Starting Lineup action figures (which often have cards) are covered in detail.

Sports Collectors Digest, 700 East State St., Iola, WI 54990

This weekly is like a huge newspaper, with more than 200 oversized pages. Being published so often means that readers might get a new set's checklist at least two weeks before a monthly magazine can release the news. SCD is known mostly for its tons of advertising. The ads range from mail-order dealers of all kinds to collectors who buy tiny classifieds trying to fill out their almost-done sets. The ads are sometimes more fascinating than the articles.

Hobby publishers are only a few sources of information that can be found on the Internet. Most on-line information is free. Again, the leader in basketball-card information would be Beckett Publications, through www.beckett.com. Some sections of the Web site are available only to registered members with passwords, although registration is free.

INTERNET SOURCES

Consider hobby expert John Raybin an "e-zine" publisher, in that his magazine-like servings of news are seen only on the Internet. His address is www.sportscollectors.com.

Should you try a search engine on the Internet-like Yahoo or Excite to find on-line sources for basketball card-related news? Your efforts may bring mixed results. It's nice to think that new leagues, companies, and publications may be starting up new Web sites all the time. But dealers, too, are springing up all over the Internet.

That means a search request for "basketball" might send you to 20 card-dealer sites, before alerting you to the truly informative stuff. It's like going to the library. A whole shelf full of books may have only one title that can help you.

BOOKS

To collect your own basketball-card information, start by thinking about a hobby library. Numerous worthwhile books are available from Beckett Publications, with new editions published regularly.

Krause Publications, SCD's maker, has also built a huge line of hobby-related books.

Both Krause and Beckett create worthy, encyclopedia-like books that retell the history of many cards and checklist whole sets, including regionals. Another helpful book, with versions created by each publisher, is an alphabetical checklist. To find out how many cards Magic Johnson was on during his career, you no longer have to leaf through a decade's worth of checklists. You can look up "Johnson, Magic," and find his card's numbers from any year he was featured.

Of course, most books about basketball cards will focus on price-guide values. But that's a risky business, hoping that a book quoting any card's value will be accurate a year later. Most collectors prefer monthly or weekly updates, or even daily briefings on card values from the Internet. The yearly price-guide books seem best for collectors wanting a complete *listing* of every card from every set ever made. That's a service that magazines don't have the time or space to provide.

ABA: American Basketball Association, which played from 1967 to 1976.

ABL: American Basketball League, female rival to WNBA.

Album: 1. A three-ring binder, to display cards kept in plastic sheets. 2. A paperback book made to display collectible stickers.

Autograph: 1. A card signed by the player shown. 2. A signed card of that player, autographed in limited quantity, certified as a real autograph by the manufacturer, then inserted in random packs. 3. A signature.

Beckett: A registered trademark of Beckett Publications. The name of price-guide founder Dr. James Beckett is used often as a guide-line for the value of a card. If a dealer will sell at "half Beckett," that means the card would cost half the listed price in *Beckett Basketball Card Monthly* magazine.

Blankback: A normal card, except that all the printing was omitted from the back. Although these cards are not common, few people buy or sell these mistakes. This limits their value. See also *Wrongback*.

Blister pack: A cardboard-backed package, designed to be hung and displayed on a store shelf. Often, some cards are visible through the plastic fronts of blister packs.

Border: A frame-like stripe surrounding the photo area on the front of a card. To be a mint card, all borders must be equal.

Bowman: A card manufacturer that published cards from 1948 to 1955. Its 1948 set was considered the first of the modern basketball hobby. Originally known as Gum, Inc., Bowman was purchased by Topps, which began issuing sets under the Bowman name in 1989.

Box: A vending container issued by card companies to be used by retailers. Usually containing 24 to 36 packs, a box may contain a bonus card, as a reward for buying all the packs.

Centered: Having an image placed properly in the middle of the card. A card with an off-center photo is not considered mint or worth top values.

Checklist: 1. A complete listing of every card in a set. 2. A card that lists part of the cards in a set. Checklists that haven't been marked or written on are worth more money.

Collectibles: 1. Cards worthy of a collector's attention. 2. Non-card items of memorabilia.

Collector: A person who collects basketball cards first for fun, without seeking to make money.

Combination card: Known as a *combo*, this is a card that represents more than one player. Often, each of the players will be identified by name on the card front.

Commemoratives: Cards that were made to highlight a certain event, such as the 50th anniversary of the NBA.

Common: One of the least-wanted cards in a set. The player depicted is not popular or in demand. As a result, the card is easy to get and affordable.

Convention: See *Show*. A convention is the largest kind of show, often lasting two or three days.

Convention issue: One or more cards produced to promote a sports collectibles show. Often, the cards are only available at that show, sometimes sold, sometimes given away. Also known as "promo" cards.

Correction: A card issued by a manufacturer to correct an error on that same card. Either version may be more or less collectible, depending on its availability.

Counterfeit: An illegally reprinted version of a card, which has no actual value but is wrongly sold as the actual card.

Dealer: A person who buys, sells, or trades collectibles to make a profit. The dealer may also collect, but making money is the first goal.

Die-cut: A card with part of its stock cut out, often to create fancy shapes.

Double-printed: Refers to a card, issued in twice the quantity as other cards. When the company printed the sheet of cards, that card appeared one extra time compared with the others.

Dream Team: A nickname given to U.S. Olympic basketball teams after NBA players were allowed to play.

Duplicate: The exact same card as another; also called a "dupe."

Error: A card with incorrect statistics, information, or photos on its front or back. Most errors go unfixed by the card companies.

Extra: Same as *Duplicate*.

Factory-collated: A set, complete and sorted, often by the manufacturer's machinery, and sold as a unit. These cards are not necessarily mint simply because they came straight from the factory.

Food issue: Cards made to help promote or sell meals or certain food products.

Franchise: A national or international company with many small, locally owned branches. Burger King is one example of a franchise.

Grade: To judge the condition of a card, looking at its creases, bent corners, or other problems. Cards graded as "mint" are worth the most money, worn cards are worth less.

Hand-sorted: Of a set of cards, complete and assembled by hand from numerous individual packages. Compare *Factory-collated*.

Hobby only: An arrangement by which manufacturers make some cards available only through packs sold by hobby shops and card dealers.

Hologram: Any of a number of specialized foil-like stickers and cards that give an image or photograph a three-dimensional appearance. Created by Upper Deck and other companies.

Insert: A card not considered part of a regular set, printed in limited quantities and randomly placed in selected packs.

Issue: 1. To make available. 2. One set from a single source, such as a "Fleer issue."

Lot: An assortment of cards, related in some way, such as the same player, team, or set. The cards are grouped as a lot (or "brick") to be sold together.

Mail-in cards: Cards that can only be obtained from the company by mail. Often, mail-in cards require money and empty card wrappers.

Manufacturer: A company creating a product. For example, Topps is a manufacturer of cards.

Memorabilia: Non-card items such as autographs, team publications, and equipment. Similar to *Collectibles*.

Miscut: A card that is removed from the large printing sheet and cut improperly. The card may not have the standard shape, and will have uneven centering.

NBA: National Basketball Association.

Odds: The chances of finding an insert card in a pack. See *Ratio*.

Olympics card: A card showing specific basketball players in Olympic competition.

Panel: Two or more individual cards attached, sometimes by a perforation. When the cards are separated from their panels, their condition and value might decrease.

Parallel cards: Cards much like regular cards except for a special touch, such as embossed or die-cut features.

Perforated: Having a dotted line, slightly cut, to show collectors where cards can be removed from a sheet. Dividing cards along perforated lines lessens their condition, though.

Premium: 1. A special card or prize offered by mail by a company. 2. Cards that have more expensive special features, such as a thicker stock. 3. Appealing, collectible cards from the past.

Promo: One or more cards used to promote a company, event, or final card set. Usually, promos are free samples, or gifts for attending a collectors' convention.

Protective page: A plasticlike sheet with pockets, used to protect and display cards, as in a three-ring notebook.

Prototype: An early design for a card, which may differ from the future set. Sometimes, these cards were given as samples. See also *Promo*.

Random: Only sometimes, or in some packs.

Rare: An overused, misused hobby term. A "rare" card is the hardest of any to find, harder to find than "scarce" cards.

Ratio: The average in which a certain insert card might be found in sealed packs. However, even when a pack says an insert ratio is 1:9 (one in nine packs), more or fewer cards could be found in those packs.

Redemption card: A card found in packs that, when mailed in, can be redeemed to obtain special cards or prizes.

Regional: Intended for distribution only in certain geographical regions. Regional card sets may focus on one team and get circulated only in the team's nearby area.

Reprint: A later printing of a card, clearly marking the new, nearly identical version of the card as a "reprint." A reprint card also may be re-created in a smaller size or a different card stock to avoid confusion among collectors. See also *Commemoratives*.

Retail only: A requirement by a company that certain cards may be sold only in retail outlets, such as Kmart or Wal-Mart.

Reverse: 1. The back side of a card, where the statistics and biography are found. 2. A photo negative turned wrongly, making the card image appear backward. In a photo reverse, uniform numbers will look backward, or a right-handed player will look left-handed.

Rookie card: A beginning player's first appearance on a regular card in a nationally issued set from a major company. A rookie card may be the player's regular card or his draft pick card. If a player doesn't appear in a certain set until years after his career begins, that card will *not* be considered a rookie card.

SASE: Self-addressed, stamped envelope, sent to help get a return reply by mail.

Scarce: See *Rare*.

SCD: *Sports Collectors Digest*, a weekly hobby publication.

Series: A grouping of a portion of cards in a set. For instance, a 400-card set may be issued in two stages, offering the first 200 cards in the first series.

Set: A grouping of cards having one of each card from a basic set, not including inserts or other specialty cards. The set of 1995–96 Upper Deck cards contains 360 cards, numbered 1 through 360.

Sheet: See *Protective page.*

Show: A location where collectors and dealers gather on the same day, in order to buy, sell, and trade cards and collectibles.

Sleeve: A card-sized plastic pouch used to protect and display one card. See *Protective page.*

Standard-size card: 2½ by 3½ inches.

Stock: The paper on which the card is printed, determining the card's thickness.

Subset: A group of cards within a regular set, such as seven cards within an NBA set honoring the NBA finals.

Team card: A card that shows a photograph of a whole team.

Team issue: Cards created and distributed by the team represented on the cards.

Team set: A collection of all cards depicting members of one team from one set. Once offered only by dealers who would hand-sort cards into teams, reselling them in groups, some companies now sell the assortments themselves.

Team USA: The official name given to each men's or women's United States basketball team competing in the Olympics.

Three-dimensional: Cards having photographs that seem to move when tilted.

Uncut sheet: A sheet containing more than one card, never cut by the manufacturer.

Variation: Another version of the same card, often the same numbered card. This can mean an error card or the corrected card. When the company finds a mistake on a card, and tries to fix the mistake, a variation happens. A variation may have one tiny, overlooked differing color or design element. A variation can be easier or harder to get than the "irregular" version of the card, depending on when each version was printed.

Wax pack: An individually wrapped pack of cards. Previously, cards came in wrappers made of waxed paper.

WNBA: Women's National Basketball Association, with teams owned by the NBA.

Wrongback: A card that contains the back of another card from that set. A wrongback is more common than a *Blankback*, but neither has a serious chance for increased value.

INDEX

Page numbers in *italics* refer to illustrations.